Living for CHRIST

Christian Devotional

ABIGAIL NISPEL

ISBN 979-8-88685-892-1 (paperback)
ISBN 979-8-88685-894-5 (hardcover)
ISBN 979-8-88685-893-8 (digital)

Christian Faith Publishing
832 Park Avenue
Meadville, PA 16335
www.christianfaithpublishing.com

Printed in the United States of America

Are You Thankful?

Each and every day we are given is a blessing. In all America, there are over 564,000 people sleeping on benches or sidewalks, while we are in a nice house, taking a hot shower every night. And yet we complain constantly! Most of the time, we are like the Israelites in the wilderness, always complaining and never being thankful for the many extraordinary blessings God gives us each day.

Every minute we breathe is a blessing, every crumb we can eat without tubes in our throat is a gift, and every friend God provides us with, we don't deserve. God is so gracious, and His mercy endureth forever. Make today your day to give God thanks for all He's done in your life, and you will find that you are more blessed than you've ever realized.

Psalm 103:8; Psalm 107

Run the Race with Patience

Everyone has a sin they struggle with the most, and for me, it's patience. Even though it is my biggest struggle, God has helped me every day to become a little more patient, but I still have many more lessons to learn. Whatever your struggle is, the Lord can help you, too, but He can only help us if we have an open heart. He wants to help us do what's right and bring Him more glory through our everyday walk, but we must want His help.

In Hebrews 12:1 the Bible says, "And let us run with patience the race that is set before us."

Every day is a battle, and in every minute is a decision, whether we're gonna keep running the race or whether we're just gonna quit. My mom's favorite movie is called *Facing the Giants*, and one of my favorite parts in it is when the coach is telling the football player "Don't quit!" When you're about to quit, just listen to God. I guarantee you He's telling you "Don't quit!" Just hold on, be patient, and fight the battle. When you get to the finish line, you'll be so glad you kept on going.

The second letter of Paul to Timothy 4:7 says this, "I have fought a good fight, I have finished my course, I have kept the faith." Don't quit! Be patient. Keep fighting. Keep stepping forward, and give God the glory.

Whether you're waiting for a spouse, a child, a job, a house, a good friend, or whatever it may be, God knows, and His way is always best, and His timing is never too late.

Just keep running, and don't quit!

The Power of Prayer

Prayer is one of our greatest blessings, and so many times, we take it for granted.

Many religions "hope" that their prayers are heard, they "hope" that they're going to heaven, but only true salvation is what gets you to heaven. True salvation is confidence in the blood of Jesus Christ alone to pay for all your sins, and you can know for sure that you are saved!

Prayer is our access to God. We talk to our Heavenly Father, our Savior, our Best Friend, through prayer. Prayer is not some long thought-out poem that we repeat many times, but prayer is simply pouring out your heart to God, knowing that He hears and He answers.

A certain friend of mine would almost always have something to share with me about how God was good, and every time I told him something I was struggling with, he'd say, "I'm praying for you." And I knew he meant that and he wasn't just saying it. If there's only one thing that you remember from this chapter, may you remember that God is good and He answers prayer. It may not always be what we want Him to say, but He knows what's best, and we just need to trust Him to give the right answer to our prayers.

On the days we are given bad news, we can cry, we can sit in silence, or we can share our burden with those around us who are willing to share the burden. But the most effective thing we can do even when our world is torn apart is pray. God knows all that happens in your heart and life, and He wants you to lean on Him and His strength through it all. Prayer is so powerful, and do you know why? Because He answers!

Trusting through the Valleys

It's not easy to trust in the Lord, but it's what we need to do as Christians. Proverbs 3:5–6 says, "Trust in the Lord with all thine heart; and lean not unto thine own understanding. In all thy ways acknowledge him, and he shall direct thy paths." Life is a long road that we travel. There are twists, turns, and sometimes fog. We may not know where we're turning next, but God does, and He'll tell us when to turn if we trust Him. There will be valleys, but we can't make it to the mountain without going through the valleys. Job had many valleys, but even though he lost everything he had on this earth, he still had hope and trust in God. He said in Job 13:15, "Though he slay me, yet will I trust in him." I'm not sure what I'd have done if I was Job, but I don't think my response would've been the same.

What would you say if you had everything in life on this earth taken away? Maybe you're going through a valley today, or maybe you're on the mountain. But wherever we are, may we put our trust in the Lord.

God's Still Faithful

Even when things go wrong, God is always faithful. In Hebrews 13:5, God promised, "I will never leave thee, nor forsake thee." God is so good, and He is always right beside us. And in every trial, every death, every problem that comes our way, He is in control, and He will never leave us! Today, I was told that a friend of mine passed away. And even though my eyes were filled with tears, I knew that God was right there beside me, and just to think about the fact that I would see her again someday in a better place gave me an unexplainable peace. Another friend of mine who is in Romania was talking to me about some things, and he said that it's good to have a place to call home. And for me, that's America, but then he said that we need to be happy with where God puts us. At that time, it seriously got me thinking of how much I discourage myself when I say, "If only we were home," instead of saying, "God placed us here. He'll help us through this." I need to be better at that. Even though life brings hardships and we feel tears at times, we can rejoice in our constant hope and our Giver of joy, Who, even in the midst of our toughest times, is with us. May we remember that even in the problems of life, God is still faithful.

Everlasting Love

Many of us can say that we love someone. Whether it's a family member or a friend, you love them. The definition of *love* is a deep care for someone, such selflessness that you would give your own life for that person. In Jeremiah 31:3, it says, "The Lord hath appeared of old unto me, saying, Yea, I have loved thee with an everlasting love: therefore with lovingkindness have I drawn thee." The love of Jesus is unending, and He will never stop loving His child, no matter what you do! Once you're saved, you're always saved. If you are a born-again believer, then you are on your way to heaven. And no one can ever take away your salvation, not even you!

Jesus gave His life for us, because He loved us. It says in 1 John 4:19, "We love him, because he first loved us."

Since I got saved, I've never felt more loved, and I will forever love Him because of how much He loves me!

Proverbs 18:24 says, "There is a friend that sticketh closer than a brother." You may know someone who is not walking as a Christian should walk, but despite how much God hates to see His children walk in darkness, God still loves them with an everlasting love, and He will never leave or forsake them. This is not to say that sin goes unpunished. God is righteous, and God is gracious. But just like a child, once he is born, he can never be unborn. A born-again child of God can never lose his salvation.

People are not perfect, so they're going to let you down. But there is a friend who sticketh closer than a brother, and He is perfect, and He will never let you down!

Jesus Christ loved you enough to die for you and then rise up from the dead! He made you for a reason, and He wants to use you. But first, you have to give Him your life. After all, He gave you His life.

Never Alone

*I*n Hebrews 13:5, Jesus said, "I will never leave thee, nor forsake thee." That's a promise! God has never broken His word, and he's not about to start! There have been times when I feel like I'm the only one who doesn't like where God's planted me, and I often feel alone and think that I don't have any friends, but it's when I read my Bible and start praying when I finally realize how wrong I am. Jesus is a friend who sticketh closer than a brother, and He is always with me, and I am never alone. If you have Jesus in your heart, you will never be alone either.

Some of you feel lonesome, but what the Lord wants you to remember is that you're never alone and that He is *always* right beside you!

I understand that having Jesus with you always is not the same as a physical human being whom you can touch and hear physically, but I believe that if a person has a close relationship with God, they will feel Him working and hear Him speaking. So may we all keep in mind that Jesus is always with us and He wants us to call out to Him whenever we feel lonely.

John 14:18; Isaiah 58:9; Isaiah 43:4; 2 Corinthians 6:18; Genesis 28:15

Communication

Too often we forget to communicate with our Heavenly Father, and I'm especially speaking to myself. Since I and my family first came to Romania as missionaries, I had wanted to talk to one of the older Romanian ladies in our church but never mustered up enough courage to start a conversation with her in Romanian. I asked God to give me the strength to talk to her, and He did. A few weeks later, I asked her what her favorite Bible verse was, and she told me. So for Christmas I made her a drawing with that verse on, and God blessed my heart through it.

The fact is God gave me the courage to talk to her! Although my bones were full of nervousness, the Lord gave me a calm spirit through it all, and He strengthened me enough to communicate with her.

We have no need to be nervous about talking to God. Hebrews 4:16 says, "Let us therefore come boldly unto the throne of grace, that we may obtain mercy, and find grace to help in time of need."

Jesus is not only your Judge and your Father, but He wants to be your Best Friend! He loved you so much, enough to die for you and then to rise up from the dead. He absolutely has your best interest at heart! He created you, and He wants to hear from you! Not just at the table before supper but throughout the day He's given you. Communicate with the One Who loves you more than anyone else ever could, and let Him strengthen your love for Him!

Praising God in the Problems

God is good, and even in the problems, we should give thanks to the God Who is with us.

Sometimes, we get upset at God for giving us the problem because we think He's just giving us the problem and then leaving us to conquer it on our own, but that is not true at all!

The whole reason He gives us the problem is so that we'll draw closer to Him while He walks us through the problem with us. He will never leave us, and He will never be unworthy of our praise!

A sermon I heard was about the problems in life, and the man preaching said something really true to life. He said that life isn't all just happiness and joy; it has problems too. When someone gets saved, the reason they're so filled with happiness and joy is because they know that when the problems do come, God is standing right beside them.

I think that the more time passes since the day we got saved, our focus becomes a little dimmed and maybe we even become distracted, but just because we've forgotten where our joy comes from doesn't mean His joy supply has gone dry. We just need to dip our hearts in His ever-abundant fountain of joy, and we need to get our focus back on Him and His Word!

Psalms is my favorite book of the Bible, because it is all songs of praise in among life's problems. Despite all the negatives the psalmist went through in his own life, the book ends with a song of praise and a call for all the earth to praise the Lord with him! This should be our motivation in our problems! Remember you cannot worry and worship at the same time.

In the movie *Fireproof* it was said, "Fireproof doesn't mean that a fire will never come, but that you'll be able to withstand the fire when it does." So remember, when problems come, draw near to the fountain of joy and fix your eyes on the Savior. And He'll guide you through the problems.

Trust God. He knows everything you're facing, and I guarantee you He knows how to get you through it.

Where Is Your Hope?

Years ago, while my family and I were in Texas, we went to a ladies' meeting at a nearby church, where two young ladies sang a song with these words in the chorus, "My hope is in the Lord. I will trust in Him, and Him alone. While death knocks at my door, my hope is in the Lord."

With those words ringing through my mind and being five thousand miles away from our family and friends, I was reminded that even though it is hard, our hope is in the Lord! We know we will see them again with the help of the Lord. Whether that's here on earth or in heaven someday, we have hope that we will see them again.

The definition of *hope* is "a feeling of expectation and a desire for a particular thing to happen, and full confidence that what we are waiting for will happen."

The Bible has a lot of verses about hope, 133 to be exact. Ask yourself this one simple question, "Where is my hope?"

Is it in the things and people of this world, or is it in the Lord Jesus Christ?

When we place our hope in physical and temporal things, we must realize that the things of this world and even the people we hope in will fail us at some point. Things will break, people will die, and hope will fade if it is not placed in the right person—Jesus Christ!

Our Great God

In Colossians 1:16, it says, "For by him were all things created, that are in heaven, and that are in earth, visible and invisible, whether they be thrones, or dominions, or principalities, or powers: all things were created by him, and for him."

We, as Christians, know that God created the universe. And if everyone were to be completely honest, they would tell you that they, too, know that there was a divine Creator; they just don't want to accept it.

What was it like when God spoke what we are, what we see, and what we live in into existence?

He just said it, and it happened! Our God is so powerful that when He says something, within a moment's time, it happens!

It is so amazing to me to know that the God Who created the heavens, and the earth, cared enough about me and you to create us even though He knew that we were going to disobey Him and then He would leave heaven to come down to earth, to be born as a baby, and to be crucified for our sins, paying our penalty, and then He would rise up from the grave, conquering death, and would ascend back into heaven with scars in His hands and feet. That just really makes me think about how much He really loves me and you, and it makes me wonder how often I show my love for Him.

The song called "He Knows My Name" is a blessing to me.

Think about it. Jesus, the Lord of everything, loves you so much that He knows your name out of all the millions of people He created, and not only does He know your name but also the number of hairs on your head and the innermost thoughts of your heart. Jesus doesn't just know you, but He is with you every single day. God is so powerful. He is the beginning and the end. He created everything! Yet even though He is so great and so powerful, He loves you, and He wants to communicate with you, and He wants you to know Him, not just as the Creator of the universe but as your very Best Friend and your Heavenly Father.

Waiting with Hope

W e have all waited for something. Whether it's a family visit that you've been waiting for a long time, whether it's a sweet little one in your family, whether it's a special someone to take part in your life, whatever it is, we've all waited for something. Some of us are still waiting, but we need to learn how to wait the right way. We need to wait with hope. Hope means to have full confidence that something you are waiting for to happen will happen!

In Psalm 40:1 it says, "I waited patiently for the Lord; and he inclined unto me, and heard my cry."

God hears your prayers, and even though it may seem like you've been waiting a lifetime for His answer, realize He's already answered! He might have said, "Trust Me while waiting. I know the plans I have for you. You just need to be still and know that I am God."

Remember that Hannah and her husband waited a long time before they had a son. Abraham and Sarah waited for what felt like a lifetime before God gave them a child, but can you imagine the joy they had when Isaac was born! They trusted God so much that they were ready to give Isaac back to the Lord even after all their difficulties with having a child. All I can say is I hope that if God asked me to do that, I would have as much hope in Him as Abraham and Sarah did.

God may be asking you to wait, and the best thing to do is wait. Even if we feel like the answer is right in front of us, we need to trust God and wait for Him to tell us it's time.

Lamentations 3:25; Psalm 31:24; Matthew 6:8
Hebrews 11:1; 2 Corinthians 5:7

Proclaiming Praise

Psalm 34:1 says, "I will bless the Lord at all times: his praise shall continually be in my mouth."

Is His praise continually in our mouths? Even if we're struggling with something, are we still giving God praise for all He has done for us? Paul and Silas were in prison, and it surely seemed like they would die, but did they stop praising God? No. Instead of saying, "Why did God put us here after all we've done for Him!" they sang praises to His holy name.

After Job lost everything he had, he said, "Though he slay me, yet will I trust in him."

We have so many things to praise the Lord for, but it seems we barely thank Him for the meals we eat and the shoes on our feet. Just because you feel like you're losing, and you have every reason to complain, doesn't mean you don't have something to praise God for.

God is so gracious, and I guarantee you that the reason we are where we are today is not because of anything we've done! It's because of His mercy and grace and because of what He's done!

Jeremiah said it best when he said in Lamentations 3:22, "It is of the Lord's mercies that we are not consumed, because his compassions fail not."

We need to continually be praising God for something, not complaining because we think we should be treated better.

God's ways are higher than our ways, and His thoughts are better than our thoughts.

Maybe this is exactly God's intention of drawing you closer to Himself. The closer we are to Him, the more blessed we feel, and the more praise flows out of our mouths.

> I will greatly praise the Lord with my mouth; yea, I will praise him among the multitude. (Psalm 109:30)

Servants of the King

*I*n 1 Samuel 3:10 it says, "And the Lord came, and stood, and called as at other times, Samuel, Samuel. Then Samuel answered, Speak; for thy servant heareth."

When God speaks to us, do we have that kind of response? If God asks us to do something for Him, do we say, "Speak, Lord, for Thy servant heareth"? Or do we have a totally different response? Since we are His workmanship—we were created by Him and for Him—therefore, our purpose is to serve Him. He's the One Who gave us life, Who gives us every breath we breathe. We ought to use it for Him! Whether it's in a foreign country or simply passing out tracts at a grocery store, it pleases God when His children want to bring Him pleasure and when they find pleasure in serving Him with all their heart.

We may not think that what we are doing for Him is making a difference. But no matter how small our service may seem, it is needed, and it brings God glory and honor. I know people who have seen hundreds of souls come to know Christ, while I myself have only heard about souls getting saved. I have never really led one to the Lord. It thrills my heart to hear about people getting saved, but I sometimes think that what I do doesn't make a difference, but that's when I need to remember you can't harvest a field of corn if no one plants it. As simple as it may sound, every field needs laborers, and not every laborer takes part in the harvest work. But each job is necessary. Without a fertile ground, the seed doesn't take root. Without water the plant withers. Without a gardener weeds take over. Without open air to the sunshine they dry up. And without the harvesters, they are never harvested.

My mom told me this, "We can't all be missionaries, or there'd be no souls to reach. We can't all be pastors, or there'd be no congregation." And it is very true.

God has a special plan for each one of His children. We just need to keep serving Him until He's ready to reveal it to us. No matter what we're doing, we can glorify God in it.

God gives everyone different gifts, because He gave everyone a different purpose. We need to serve God with the gifts He's given us.

Not only should we serve the Lord but we should serve the Lord with gladness.

Psalm 100:2 says, "Serve the Lord with gladness: come before his presence with singing."

If we don't have a good heart when we serve the Lord, it won't please Him. God loves a cheerful giver. Many times we apply this to money only. But I believe it can be applied to the giving of time, labor, and service.

The Bible tells us that we are no longer slaves in bondage to fear, but we are servants of the King, and we are freed from the chains of the law.

If the King returns today, would we be ready? Would He say, "Well done, my good and faithful servant."? Or would He say, "I wish you would've served Me and experienced all the blessings in serving Me rather than your own flesh"? We need to serve the King and be ready for His coming!

A Shelter in a Time of Storm

In the times when we think that God is not able to help us through a storm, we fail to listen to God as He is calmly whispering, "Do you not remember where I brought you from? Just take a look behind you and at how far you've come. So why would you be thinking that I would not see you through?"

Jesus walked on the water, and He calmed the raging sea by saying just three words. He spoke to the wind; it hushed and gave peace. He hears us when we call and catches us when we fall. He left heaven, to sacrifice His life for the sins of the world. He knew we wouldn't love Him, but He still loved us anyway. He conquered the grave, and yet we think that He can't help us through the trials that He brings into our life! We often forget that God is the One Who gives us problems, but He gives them for a reason. If we never had problems, we would never know what He's able to do! Our God is faithful, and His hand is stretched out to you to pull you from the raging waters around you and speak peace into your troubled heart!

I know that problems are not easy, but they are so much easier when we trust God through it. Many times, God gives us problems because He knows that it is the only way we'll draw closer to Him. The Lord is a place of refuge in a storm, He's the answer to every problem, and He wants us to trust Him in times of storm and times of peace!

Psalm 107:29; Psalm 9:9; Psalm 46

Never-Changing God

*H*ebrews 13:8 says, "Jesus Christ the same yesterday, and to day, and for ever."

In life, you will meet many people, and you will have many friends, but we must always put our hopes and dreams in Jesus Christ. People change, life changes, and we ourselves even change. But the Lord never changes! Jesus was, is, and will forever be the King of kings, Prince of peace, and Lord of lords. And He will never grow weary!

Ephesians 2:4 says, "But God, who is rich in mercy, for his great love wherewith he loved us." Jesus is a never-changing God, Whom we can lean on, and we can stand upon the Rock of ages!

Just like He healed the lame, loved the unloved, and calmed the raging seas, He is still able to do the possible and the impossible! Yet we still question His ability! Whenever we start to doubt if He can do something, we need to remember what He has already done. He willingly gave His own life for yours, He gloriously rose up from the grave, and many of us can say that He has saved our souls from the lowest hell and has blessed us beyond measure!

In our lives, we have many choices, and we change our minds very often. But Jesus never changes His mind. Once you make the decision to ask Jesus to save you, His faithfulness endures till the end, and His mind is made up that you are bought with a price and you are His for all eternity! Our God is a never-changing God, and that's something we can always be thankful for!

Answers to Prayer

The Lord hears our cries, and He answers our prayers. Sometimes He says yes, sometimes His answer is wait, and sometimes He says no. When He says yes, we need to thank Him. When He says to wait, we need to thank Him for the time He's given us to learn patience. When He says no, we need to be grateful that He's keeping us from whatever danger only He can see. He says no because He loves us and He only wants what's best for us.

He can see our future, and He knows where we need to turn to fulfill His purpose for our lives. There's no shortcut. We need to follow Him and trust His direction, not get out our own GPS and follow our own instincts! We don't know better than He does. He knows what's best! We are not God; He is. And if we truly want to do what's best, we will surrender to His guiding hand!

The greatest blessings of life are only found in the path of following Him. By taking our own shortcuts, we miss the blessings, and we miss the peaceful journey that the Lord wants to share with us. Even in the darkest night, when you've cried all your tears and prayed about everything your heart can possibly pray for, just know that God hears and God always answers.

Listen for His whisper; reach for His peace.

Psalm 37:7; Proverbs 3:5–6; Isaiah 55:8–9; Psalm 37:23; Jeremiah 33:3

To Have Faith

"Now faith is the substance of things hoped for, the evidence of things not seen," Hebrews 11:1 states.

To have faith is hard, especially since faith is believing in something you can't see instead of something visible. Just because we can't physically see the Creator doesn't mean He doesn't exist or care. His Word is enough evidence that He cares, and all creation sings the song of their Creator. Through faith we know that He does exist because we are His workmanship and we live in His marvelous creation! What better proof do we need?

When we turn on a light switch, we are already stepping forward into the room because we have faith that it will turn on as it's supposed to, even though we don't know for sure that it will shine.

When Jesus healed the sick during His time here on earth, He healed them because they had faith. Mark 10:52 says, "And Jesus said unto him, Go thy way; thy faith hath made thee whole. And immediately he received his sight, and followed Jesus in the way." Bartimaeus was blind, so he couldn't see anything, yet he received his sight because of his faith! In Matthew 8:26, we see men in a storm with Jesus, the Master of the wind. But yet they had little faith. My question for us today is, How is our faith? Are we like the disciples in the storm with little faith, or are we like the blind man who received his sight because of his great faith? Just like blind Bartimaeus received his sight because of his faith in Jesus Christ, one day our faith will be made sight when we come into the presence of our Lord and Savior and see Him face-to-face.

Jesus wants us to have faith in Him and to trust Him in every aspect of our lives.

The question is, Do we?

Living a Testimony

Some people get saved but never fully live their life for God. They hold back, so throughout the years, they forget to grow in the Lord, and they become satisfied with being baby Christians. They draw close to those things or people they didn't remove from their daily life when the Lord told them to. God is not pleased with this, but that does not mean that He stops loving His child.

When born-again believers sin, they know they're going against God, and they know what they should do. Yet they still follow the pleasures of this world, which are only for a season.

We as Christians should live our life for Jesus and have a testimony to those around us. Maybe then they will see the blessings and the real joy in serving the Lord and the eternal rewards in following the Savior.

How are we living as Christians? Can the world see Jesus in us, or can they see someone who says they're a Christian but lives like a lost person? Most importantly, how is our testimony before the Lord? God sees you even when no one else is around, and He knows what consumes your thoughts and your heart. Is it pleasing to Him, or does it grieve His heart?

The Father's Delight

When we think of God, we often think of Him as the omniscient, omnipotent, omnipresent Creator, Savior, and King. Yes, He is all these things, but He is also our Heavenly Father if we have accepted Him as our Savior.

A father loves his child, even though the child may not think he loves them when the father corrects the child. He doesn't love the child any less; he is only doing his duty as a father.

Proverbs 3:12 says, "For whom the Lord loveth he correcteth; even as a father the son in whom he delighteth."

Just like a child hugs a toy and says with a smile, "He's mine!" so does Jesus when He looks down on His children and sees them living for Him.

Is the Lord precious to us? Is His will important in our lives, or does it not matter to us to do what pleases Him? Do we truly love Him every day of the week or just on Sunday? We all need to show our love for God more. We only have one life to live for Christ, and that life will soon be past. No one is promised tomorrow, but we have this moment, to live for Christ today and to make Him our delight.

Waiting and Praying

*H*ave you ever wondered why God keeps certain things from you but not from others?

There are things you are praying for right now that someone else has, and all you can do when you see that person holding the most precious thing that you are longing for right now to call your own is to cry out to God asking why!

You've heard it said that God doesn't withhold anything good from His children, but yet here you stand, waiting with open and empty hands.

I think that Hannah's heart felt this same way at some point in her life, before Samuel arrived. All she wanted was a child. She wanted to raise that child to do the will of God, and she wanted to walk through life holding a little hand in hers, but all she could do was wait and pray for something she had yet to see.

She did not give up hope, but she kept praying to the God of the impossible. We see that when she prayed, her heart was so sore and her cries felt so desperate, but she still poured out her soul to the Lord. Even when Eli first thought she was drunk, she didn't let others disrupt her prayer life. Hannah did not keep her heartache from God, but we see that she told the Lord of her sorrow and asked Him to deliver her from her affliction and the bitter darts from her adversary.

We get the impression that God answered her prayer quickly, but we do not know for sure how long she had to wait before having a child.

Some of us have something we're praying for so desperately. But we are still waiting, still hoping, still trying to dodge all the arrows of doubt the devil shoots at our hearts.

Let God's Word encourage you today, as we read the last words in verse 20: "and the Lord remembered her."

Just as God remembered Hannah, God remembers you, and He cares so much for you! He does not delight in your tears, but it does delight His heart when you draw nigh to Him.

Many times, we think that if God would just answer all our petitions, our life would be so much better and we would sing songs of thanksgiving all day, every day. But God knows better than that. He knows that in order for us to praise Him, we must daily see how much we need Him. We can praise the Lord for the simple fact that He hears and He cares.

We don't have to wait to praise the Lord until we have the answer to our prayers, but we can praise the Lord even more when we offer unto God the sacrifice of thanksgiving when it is truly a self-sacrifice to humble ourselves and say, "Not my will, but Thine be done."

To wait with a heart of hope is wonderful, but to pray waiting for something that we have entrusted into God's hands is even more glorious! God is glorified when the circumstances we're in make the answer to our prayers seem impossible, until God steps in, in His timing, His way, and blesses those who trust in Him!

Whatever you are waiting for today, and so desperately praying for, may we surrender our desires to God. May we also remember to never give up on hope but to wait with a thankful heart for the blessings we have now and the blessings we trust God has in store.

The answer to our prayers may not always come the way we want it or in the time we want it, but God's Word assures us that He is good and that He will reward those who wait upon Him with hope and He will not withhold any good thing from those who seek Him with a pure heart.

May we keep our heart's desire fixed on Jesus and our eyes on the blessings we hold now, as we wait for the promised return of our gracious Lord and King, Who loves us beyond our own understanding and Who wants to bless us with a stronger faith and confidence in His will and timing for the answers to our prayers.

No matter how much our heart is yearning for what we do not have, may we daily grow to have a heart full of trust that God knows what's best and He still does the impossible when we least expect it.

Matthew 7:11

He Will Provide

od has provided, is providing, and will provide. Not only does He provide our needs but also, many times, our wants. Maybe not all of them, but if we had all our wants fulfilled, we wouldn't want God. And without God, there is no life nor purpose for life. We often think that we can make it on our own, but without God, we'd fail even more. We need the Lord.

It is by His wondrous love and grace that we are here today with our needs met and our blessings abundantly supplied.

Look around. Everything that you see, every blessing, both big and small, they belong to Jesus! How can we ever think that God is not able to provide for us? It is impossible for us to have a need that the Lord cannot meet. Our Father owns the cattle on a thousand hills, and it is His delight to provide for His children. Psalm 24:1 says, "The earth is the Lord's, and the fulness thereof; the world, and they that dwell therein." We are His, and we are bought with a price.

We are His creation and His delight, and God wants us to trust in His power alone to provide our every need. He wants us to let Him form us into the masterpiece He created us to be. We need to let Him be the Potter and allow Him to mold and shape us the way He knows is best.

Abraham was ready to sacrifice his only son because he trusted God so much. He trusted that God would provide, and God did.

Even when Hagar had to leave Abraham's family and go out into the wilderness with her son Ishmael, the Lord provided water for them to drink, even after Ishmael had mocked Isaac, God's promised seed to Abraham. I see God's mercy and gracious provision when I read that!

God will provide what we need, when He sees fit. We can never understand things the way God can or even why He would love us so much to bless us and provide for us, but we must have faith in the Lord of heaven and earth and remember that the Lord will provide!

A Soul's Worth

Luke 15:7 says, "I say unto you, that likewise joy shall be in heaven over one sinner that repenteth."

There is an average of 7.8 billion people in the entire universe, and not near enough of those souls are saved and on their way to heaven, but the good news is that Jesus came to die on the cross for the sins of the entire world and to conquer the grave three days later. He loves us not because of what we can do but because of what He did! Salvation is a free gift to all, not something we can earn. Christ offers eternal life to anyone who believes in Him! He died for the homeless, the brokenhearted, the rich, the poor, doctors, nurses, firefighters, soldiers, lawyers, and even those who sweep the streets. Jesus came to seek and to save that which was lost, and that means everyone!

The second letter of Paul to Peter 3:9 tells us that the Lord is not willing that any should perish but that all should come to repentance. Unfortunately, not everyone accepts this free and wonderful gift. Some think they can earn it, while some think they can change it. Some ignore it, and some just simply reject it. The reason anyone would reject such great salvation escapes me. But no matter what their excuse is, one thing's for sure, and that is that it will not stand up before the Lord! There is one way of salvation, and that is through Jesus Christ alone and nothing else.

Psalm 49:8 states, "For the redemption of their soul is precious, and it ceaseth for ever."

You may feel like you're worth nothing, people may treat you like you don't matter, and you might think that Jesus doesn't care about you. But let me tell you that God does love you and He knows everything about you, even the number of hairs on your head! You are precious in the sight of the Lord! He died so that your soul can go to heaven, and He arose because He doesn't want you to go to hell.

He loves you! Even though we don't deserve it, He loves us, and His mercy overflows upon us each and every day.

When one sinner repents, there is joy all over heaven. The angels rejoice, the grandparents and great-grandparents rejoice even louder, and the God of heaven is overjoyed that the one He loves finally asks for the precious gift of salvation!

What is most important to the Lord is not gold or silver or material things, but it is our souls! His delight is your soul, and He longs for you to come to Him!

If you do not know the Lord as your personal Savior and are not trusting in what He did alone, let me greatly encourage you to ask God to save you today! Tomorrow may be too late. Jesus is waiting to receive you into His arms as His child. Trust Him today, and I guarantee you you'll *never* regret it!

John 3:16; Romans 5:8; Romans 3:23; Romans 10:9–13; Luke 19:10

Never Too Busy

The first letter of Paul to the Corinthians 10:31 says, "Whether therefore ye eat, or drink, or whatsoever ye do, do all to the glory of God."

Many people are too busy for God because they're too busy with the things of this life, but we should be so busy serving God and doing what He wants us to do that we're too busy to take part in the things of this world. If we make the Lord our focus and ask Him to give us the desires He wants us to have, then we will put His plans for our life first, instead of our own.

Jesus is never too busy for us! He left His throne in glory to come down to earth even though He knew how He would be treated by the people He would suffer and die for.

He hears our prayers, and He answers them. He makes time for us, and yet we put Him off to the side, and so many times we push Him away until "tomorrow." We need to make time for Him now, before it's too late! Today is the day to serve Him, because if Jesus comes back tomorrow, we will regret not giving Him all our days.

The Lord wants to hear from us, just like a father wants to hear from his children. Not only do we need to make time to pray but we need to make time to listen to what God says in His Word. We have every answer to every question that could ever fill our minds in God's Word. Every word in our Bible is there for a reason, and God preserved the words He wanted us to have today for a reason. The Bible needs to fully remain God's Word! People have created so many "new and improved" Bibles, but what they really are is new and improved to fit man's thoughts instead of God's love letter to us! When we use a false Bible, we might be pleasing many of our friends and even our own flesh, but we are definitely not pleasing the Lord when we treat what man has turned into a lie as God's true words to all mankind! We should make more time to read what God has to say to us in His Word, instead of trying to please others by dishonoring Christ. The

Lord has so much to say to us, but if we never open His Word, how will we hear from Him? The Holy Spirit surely brings things to our remembrance, but what if we have never even read what we are to remember? We need to put our armor on and pick up our two-edged sword and let it pierce our hearts to hear the voice of God in our lives.

We all have friends who are closest to us, and we call them best friends. God gives them to us so we can encourage them to live for the Lord, but we also need to realize that Jesus is our Best Friend and we need to talk to Him as much as we talk to our best friend on earth.

Let me encourage you to use each breath to glorify God! There's a song that says, "If I had but one breath, I'd use it to praise Him with!" What would we do if we only had one breath? Would we praise God for giving it to us, or would we complain that we were only given one breath?

May we never be too caught up in this life to serve the Lord.

Psalm 63:3; Proverbs 27:17

Praying in Love

I'm sure we have all been in the situation where we want to pray for someone but haven't the slightest idea of how to pray for them. What we can do is pray for protection, wisdom, health, and provision and that the Lord would give them Christian friends so they can grow closer to Him and they can encourage their friends to live for Jesus.

Sometimes we are so burdened that we think it's too hard to pray, but that's when we need to pray most! In 1 Peter 5:7, the Bible says, "Casting all your care upon him; for he careth for you." Jesus wants us to tell Him our deepest thoughts. Even if it hurts a little to take them off our own shoulders, we will feel as though we've laid down our heaviest burden and can now journey so much easier.

Psalm 73:16–17 says, "When I thought to know this, it was too painful for me; Until I went into the sanctuary of God; then understood I their end." Once we give our cares to our Heavenly Father, we will understand what peace is; and if it's God's will, He can fix those heavy burdens into light masterpieces, and He can display them as blessings in our life if we continue to walk life's long journey with our burdens surrendered to Christ.

Even when we find ourselves crying out to God, with a heart overwhelmed for the person we are praying for, we must never forget to thank God for His ever-present help and His promise to listen to our cries! He brought this person into our life for a reason, and we should be thanking God for using that person to draw us closer to Him! In life there will be people we dislike and people whom we deeply love, and we need to lift one another up in prayer. May we lay our burdens, fears, and cares at the throne of grace, knowing that the God of heaven hears our hearts and knows our prayers before we even speak.

2 Thessalonians 3:1; Ephesians 1:6

Only God

There are 4,200 religions in the world, and yet there is only one true way to get to heaven, and that is through Jesus Christ.

Although many people think that Christianity is a religion, it's a relationship. The Bible isn't just a book as people may say; it's the Holy Word of God. It doesn't matter how many people try to convince you that Jesus was a prophet; Jesus is the Son of God. God doesn't look at your church attendance, how much tithes you give, or how many tracts you pass out; He looks at your heart! We could be unsaved and yet go to church every Sunday, tithe, and pass out tracts every day and still not go to heaven, because God makes salvation very clear to us in His Word in Ephesians 2:8–9, "For by grace are ye saved through faith; and that not of yourselves: it is the gift of God: Not of works, lest any man should boast." It's not what we do that saves; it's what Jesus did on the cross because of His great love for us! The Bible also makes it clear how we can get saved in Romans 10:9–13, which is simply summed up in verse 13 when it says, "For whosoever shall call upon the name of the Lord shall be saved." Have you asked God to save you from your sins, acknowledging that He is the only way to heaven? This is my prayer for all of you, because anything else you are trusting in will only bring you to eternity in hell forever. Jesus is the only way, and I hope that is where your hope is today.

In many romance movies that we watch, it seems to always be someone in the story who dies. These of course are just movies and are not real, but Jesus's love for us is a true story. And when He died on the cross, He took the sins of the entire world upon Himself, completely covering the debt we owed. After three days, His powerful love conquered the grave, and He is alive forevermore! I guarantee you you'll never see a movie where the person comes back to life like our wonderful Savior did! Praise the Lord for that!

Jesus has done so much for us, and yet we are so ungrateful and disrespectful! What respect do we have for God? People go to church because they think it looks good. They sing praises to His holy name to fit in to the church crowd, not even thinking about the words. When someone asks us if we're Christians, what do we say? Are we proud to say yes, or would we rather say no? Do the people around us have enough evidence to even ask if we are a Christian?

It's so sad to hear someone who is a child of God take His name in vain and use it as a curse word. That makes Jesus very unhappy. Let me ask you this, If Jesus were to ask us if we love Him, what would we say? Some of us might say no, some of us might say yes and live up to our words, and yet very many of us would say yes and act as if we've never said those words. He is the King of kings, Lord of lords, God of gods, and Righteous Judge! We all need to respect the Lord more, and we can start by loving Him more. The best way to grow more in love with Jesus is to spend time with Him and to look back at all He's done for us.

Only God knows what tomorrow will bring, only God knows everything about you, only God can do the impossible, only God heals the incurable, and only salvation through Him alone is what saves sinners from spending eternity in hell. John 14:6 says this, "Jesus saith unto him, I am the way, the truth, and the life: no man cometh unto the Father, but by me."

What are you trusting in to get you to heaven? Is it a religion or a relationship with the Creator of all that is? He is the only way to get to heaven. Anything else will get you to hell. We only have one life to live for Christ. Are we living for Him?

James 1:26; Proverbs 30:5; Psalm 4:8; Psalm 62:2; Psalm 62:5–6; Matthew 4:10; Matthew 6:24

Guard Your Heart

Proverbs 4:23 says, "Keep thy heart with all diligence; for out of it are the issues of life."

Everything that we think, say, and do begins in our heart. God mentions the heart 884 times in His Word, so it truly must be important. Loving Jesus starts with the heart. Then we put that love into our words and then our actions. In Matthew 6:21, Jesus said, "For where your treasure is, there will your heart be also." Love isn't the only thing that starts in our hearts. Sin begins in the heart as well, and if we aren't carefully guarding our hearts and keeping them clean, sin can very easily enter our hearts as a parasite ready to destroy all good things within us. We must destroy it and not give place to the devil to bring shame to the name of Christ and ultimately shame to us when we stand before our Redeemer.

Instead of loving worldly things and wanting to please our own selves, we need to love the Lord with all our heart, soul, and mind. If we don't keep our hearts clean, we will end up following the way of destruction. So when we find sin in our heart, we need to scrub out all the bad stuff to make room for Jesus's ways. We need to love Jesus with our whole heart, not just a part of it. Remember we can never love Jesus more than He loves us, and love starts in our hearts.

What are we letting in to our hearts?

Mark 7:21–23; Psalm 119:2; Proverbs 3:5–6

God Still Does the Impossible

There may be something we're worried about financially, but the good news is we don't have to worry. God will provide how He sees fit and when He wants to, but we must never question His ability. He does the impossible. Surely He is able to do what He knows is best for us! We need to trust Him more, because no matter how hard it seems, no matter how much money the bill says, God can make a way if it's His will. He's never failed, and He's not going to start today! God sees those who are faithful in tithing and who are good stewards of what God's given them, and in God's perfect timing He rewards them and He proves His faithfulness when we least expect it!

Everything we have, everything we are, every meal we eat, every thread of clothes on our back, *it's all God's*! It was never ours to begin with; it will always be God's! He is the One Who gives us our home and the ones in. He is the One Who gives us health, a job, and a car. And He is the One Who gives us everything that we have! May we use it in a way that is pleasing to Him.

Jesus said in Acts 20:35, "It is more blessed to give than to receive." If we are faithful to God, then He will bless us, and it's always more than we deserve. We don't deserve anything God gives us, but we can humbly give Him thanks for all that He provides and encourage others that God is faithful to His children and will provide our needs!

So whatever it is that you're facing, never forget Who Jesus is, what He's done for you, and what He can and will do if you ask Him. God still does the impossible, no matter how big the bill is!

Our Lord is powerful, and He can provide every one of our needs! We just have to trust Him.

Sometimes we may see a way that we can pay the bill ourselves, but oftentimes that means skipping church to go to work or getting a better-paying job that we know the Lord would not be pleased with. That's when Proverbs 3:5–6 comes in: "Trust in the Lord with all thine heart; and lean not unto thine own understanding. In all thy ways acknowledge him, and he shall direct thy paths." We need to trust in the Lord's knowledge, instead of our own, no matter how hard it may be. It's the right thing to do.

Ecclesiastes 1:11; Hebrews 6:8; Acts 20:35

The Perfect Love Letter

Proverbs 30:5–6 says, "Every word of God is pure: he is a shield unto them that put their trust in him. Add thou not unto his words, lest he reprove thee, and thou be found a liar."

Today, there are so many versions of the Bible, but there is only one true Word of God. Everyone is convicted differently by the Holy Spirit, and as you've probably already noticed, I use the King James Version. When God says that every word is pure, He means every word, not just every other word. He preserved what He wanted us to have. And yet, so many people try to change it to say what they want it to say, but the true and holy Word of God never changes, and what God says is what He means. He doesn't make mistakes. We do, which also shows that if God wanted to change the Bible, He would do it, not us, because if we did it, it wouldn't be holy. But praise the Lord that He hasn't changed. And He will always be the same yesterday, today, and forever, as will His Word!

As a missionary, my dad preaches at many churches, and one thing he said in one of his sermons was that God loves us so much that not only did He send His only Son to die for our sins and to rise again on the third day but He gave us a love letter. And many of us don't read it!

God preserved everything He wanted us to know, so we can learn from His Word and share this great love letter with a lost and dying world. As we see the world around us, we see how much wickedness is coming to the surface, and this should make us look at our own lives and how much we are sharing God's amazing redemption story with those who need redemption. It is so important to have a testimony that pleases God and that leads people away from the world and toward Christ, but if our testimony is no different than the world's, how can we be a witness for Christ? In many countries, they're not allowed Bibles or even to pray, and I'm sure that many of those people want to know Jesus loves them. They want to know how they can have eternal life in heaven. They want to be able to go to church. And yet here we are. We have all the freedom we could ever ask for, all the Bibles that could ever be printed, and yet what do we do with them? We need to live for Jesus more, we need to tell more people about Him, and we need to dig into the scriptures like a boy searching for treasure. May we never forget how blessed we are to have a true and living Savior Who loves us. And may we read our Bible more, for it is powerful, precious, and holy!

Hebrews 4:12

For All God's Goodness

Love is sacrifice, giving of oneself, putting the other person's needs before your own. And it is an act of selflessness and humility.

Love. God's love for us is the exact kind of love we are all looking for. Although the world may have many opinions on what love really means and how to know if it's "true love" or not, we can know without a doubt that the only opinion that matters is God's, and He showed us what love really means by His humility—by giving of Himself and by giving us eternal life when He willingly paid the highest price one could pay.

The Bible says that God is love. Since He is the very definition of love, we should get to know Him better and learn how to show that same love to other people.

God's love for us is not measured by the things we own or how many dollar bills fill up our wallet or even by what kind of home we were brought up in, but God's love for all mankind was shown at Calvary. There is no clearer picture of God's love for you than the love He humbly and compassionately displayed on the cross. God loves you and me just as much as He loves the drunk who sleeps on the streets. God loves the preacher just as much as He loves the lost sinner in the last pew. God's love for us is undeniable, and we cannot be separated from it. The only thing that can separate us from the love of God is absolutely nothing, according to Romans.

So many of us are blessed by the hand of God, and yet we feel as if God has forsaken us, because we didn't get what we wanted when we wanted it.

I have felt God's blessings on my life so much just over the period of a few short months, and I am so overwhelmed and amazed by how plenteous His love and grace is! The immeasurable amount of provision that He has done for me surpasses my understanding, but the only thing that I can do to repay Him is to praise Him! When

God blesses us, He finds pleasure in it mostly because we give Him the praise He deserves! We deserve nothing, yet He gives us so much.

We should give Him our praise in return, not because He requires it for salvation or for preservation but because it is how we can please Him and bring Him glory. He pleases us by providing for us, and we please Him by praising Him for His goodness! That fellowship is sweeter every time we raise a hallelujah for what He's done for us, whether it's what we asked for or not. God knows what we need, and He only gives us what's best. Sometimes what's best isn't what's easiest, but with God all things are possible, and with God we have everything we need.

For all God's goodness extended to us in our unworthiness, may we always remember to praise Him!

It's Still the Blood

Today, the world tries so hard to remove the blood from our songs, our Bibles, and our everyday lives. But they will never succeed at taking the blood from Jesus Christ and those who've been covered by His blood. No matter how hard people try to say the blood can no longer save a hell-bound soul, no matter how hard they try to convince the world that it's illegal to talk about it, the blood of Jesus can still cleanse us deeper than the scars of our sins can wound us! When a soul gets washed in the blood of Jesus and gets saved by God's grace alone, it may displease the people of this world, but the Bible says in Luke 15:10, "Likewise, I say unto you, there is joy in the presence of the angels of God over one sinner that repenteth." I guarantee you if you give God your heart, He'll fix everything, but you have to give Him your whole heart in order for Him to complete it. God doesn't just save bad sinners. He doesn't just save good sinners or black sinners or white sinners, but He saves whosoever will call upon the name of the Lord!

When the death angel was going to go through the land of Egypt, Jesus said, "When I see the blood, I will pass over you." God didn't say when I see your parents. He didn't say when I see your bank account or when I see what you can do. He said when I see the blood!

As Christians, we know what the blood can do! The Bible says that the life is in the blood! Praise the Lord that through the blood of Jesus we have eternal life! We experience its saving power every day, and we can face tomorrow because He lives. It didn't end at Calvary; that's where it began! Jesus willingly came down to this sin-sick world to die on the cross of Calvary and to rise again, conquering death and the grave.

To those of you who don't know Jesus as your personal Savior, you will never find what you're looking for to completely and forever satisfy your longings. In this world, everything around us will vanish away, but one thing I know for sure is that Jesus makes all the difference and He will satisfy your longing soul if you come to Him! He paid the price that we can never pay, because He loves us! He will never walk out on us, He'll never lie to us, and He'll never say we're too lost to be saved! The first letter of Paul to John 1:9 says, "If we confess our sins, he is faithful and just to forgive us our sins, and to cleanse us from all unrighteousness." It's still the blood of Jesus that is the *only* remission of sins. He knows what you need, and He holds it all. Let Him hold you, and let Him fill your heart with peace and joy and everlasting life!

God's love is so great we can't fully understand it. "Greater love hath no man than this, that a man lay down his life for his friends," John 15:13 says. May we never stop thanking God for His great love and the precious blood that He shed for our salvation.

Stepping Forward

So many times we pray that the world would change and that every living person would serve God, and we ask the Lord for people who are willing to take a stand for Him. But it will never happen if nobody starts, just like a race can never start if no one takes a step forward.

You might be the only one to have the courage to do something for God. You may be the only person willing to say, "I believe, whatever the cost." The change we've been praying for, God's calling you and me to be that change. We need to be willing to say, "Here am I, Lord. I'm yours to do with as You wish!"

I've had a song playing through my head. It's called "Let It Start in Me," and I want to be brave enough for my Savior to live those words. We all need to step up and take a stand for Jesus, even if we're the first one to step forward. We can never give the Lord more than He gave us. Jesus humbled himself for us sinners. Surely we should humble ourselves for our living King and Savior!

God has done so much for us. We should never be ashamed to do something for Him. Are we willing to step forward for Christ? We should be willing to step out for Him, and just watch. He'll walk right beside you.

Romans 1:16; Psalm 31:1; Psalm 119:46; Philippians 1:21; 1 Corinthians 10:31

Walking by Faith

Before sin entered the world, Adam and Eve walked with God physically and spiritually. And it was wonderful, until they made the choice to sin against God, by eating of the tree of knowledge of good and evil. Once sin entered the world, they could no longer walk in the beautiful garden of Eden. God didn't let them stay there, because then it wouldn't be wonderful or beautiful anymore, but that didn't mean God stopped loving them. He killed an innocent lamb to cover their sin, until one day Jesus would come to earth to pay their sin debt in full. He still loved them, but He hated the sin they had committed and couldn't let them live forever with sin.

After they had to leave the garden, God blessed them with children, and then He blessed them with grandchildren, and so on.

From Genesis to Revelation, we see God's love and His faithfulness to His children! Just as He promised in His Word, God sent His only Son to die for the sins of the world and provide a way for us to have everlasting life in heaven with Him, where there's no sin, no death, and no crying or pain and where we will worship the Lord our God for all eternity!

As Christians, we are still awaiting the return of our Savior, to take us to heaven and deliver us from this sin-cursed world, and we believe through faith that He will come back for us!

Our true and living God has kept His promises since day one. And He's not going to start breaking promises today, tomorrow, or one hundred years from now!

As Christians, we can rest in the presence of God in our lives, find peace in the midst of war, and have hope when all around us crumbles. We can lay our burdens at His feet and feel His rest all day long. The favorite part of our day should be the time we set aside to spend with the Lord.

Noah had a close walk with God. And when God told him to build an ark because it was going to rain, rather than heeding to the world's jeers and calling God crazy, he obeyed what God told him to do. And in the end, he was blessed. Noah had no idea what rain was. He never saw such a thing, but yet he had so much faith in God that he didn't let the world come between him and God, and Noah still walked with God faithfully.

What would you have done if you were Noah? Would you have built the ark knowing that something you had never seen before would fall from the sky, destroying the entire population that was not in the ark? Or would you have given in to the world's mocking and stopped walking by faith in God?

Shadrach, Meshach, and Abednego were cast into a fiery furnace. And when they came out, not one thread of their clothing was singed, nor did they even smell like smoke! God brought them through that fire, proving to all the people that He was stronger than the Babylonians were! Shadrach, Meshach, and Abednego's trust in Jesus Christ was so strong that they were ready to die because of their walk with God! God protected them in the fire, and that same God is our refuge and strength and our very present help in trouble. We all need to have a closer walk with the Lord and remember that even when what He calls us to do seems crazy, God's ways are higher than ours and His power is infinite. Walk by faith, walk with God, and never stop.

Deuteronomy 10:12; Isaiah 40:31; Daniel 3

Faithful to His Promises

When we read through the Bible, we see the fingerprints of God on every page! We see how He was faithful to His people and how He had so much mercy. We read of His promise to Abraham and then see it fulfilled. We also learn of the Lord's promises to us as Christians, and some of those promises are fulfilled every day, like His promise to never leave us nor forsake us or His promise that if we seek Him, we'll find Him. If I were to write of all His faithfulness, it would take an eternity.

As we look at His faithfulness in the past and in the present, how could we think that He'll fail us in the future? We know that God keeps His promises, and oftentimes we still question if He's still faithful. But in Hebrews 13:8 it says, "Jesus Christ the same yesterday, and to day, and for ever." That means He's just as faithful now as He was in the beginning of time!

We're also told in another verse that "the Lord is not slack concerning his promises"!

What an encouragement that our God will not suffer His faithfulness to fail. No matter how bad our life gets, He remains the same.

The second letter of Paul to the Corinthians 4:18 says, "While we look not at the things which are seen, but at the things which are not seen: for the things which are seen are temporal; but the things which are not seen are eternal."

So many people today worry so much about the things around us, but we shouldn't worry about the visible things around us because none of it will last forever and everything that we see right now is going to burn up some day. We as Christians have so much more waiting for us, things that will last forever, heavenly things, things that we cannot see right now but one day will.

On the days when we are discouraged, we should stop what we are doing and pray and ask the Lord to encourage us. Whether that is through His Word, His spirit, or a simple phone call or text message received, ask the Lord to encourage you, and reach out for His hand.

Like most people, I am not the most patient person in the world, and I get impatient all too often. This is wrong of me, and I pray that God continues to teach me patience every day. When we get impatient with the Lord and His perfect timing, which deep down we know is best but we still want to see the action now and right this second, may we remember Acts 1:7, which says, "And he said unto them, It is not for you to know the times or the seasons, which the Father hath put in his own power." Ecclesiastes 3:1–11 is also a great passage of Scripture about times.

Our God is more wonderful than we give Him credit for! There's a very special place where God wants your heart before giving you a certain desire of your heart, and He knows just when to give it to you, but we need to be patient and rejoice in the fact that Jesus makes everything beautiful in His time.

Galatians 6:9 says, "And let us not be weary in well doing: for in due season we shall reap, if we faint not." So may we run our race with patience and remember that if we keep our eyes focused on the Lord, He'll bring us to the finish line in His perfect timing having experienced all the blessings He's given along the way.

There is a poem called "The Weaver," which explains how right now we are all living a life from the back of the tapestry, but one day God will bring us to the other side and show us how beautiful He created our life and each season of it. We will stand amazed by the grace and beauty of the Lord's hand in every part of our lives!

He will finish what He has begun, and He will remain faithful to all His promises!

Ecclesiastes 3:1–11; 2 Thessalonians 3:3–5; Psalm 86:15

What Is Our Goal?

We all have some sort of goal, something that motivates us to get up in the morning, something we want to accomplish by a certain time period. While some people are enthusiastic about sports and some people have goals, such as success, money, working, or other material things, what should our goal be as Christians? Our goal should simply be to please the Lord with our life. We should be enthusiastic about doing His will, and what should motivate us to get out of bed each morning is to glorify and honor God with each day He so graciously gives us! We are so unworthy of life itself, but yet because God loved us so much, He gave us not only life on earth but the free gift of eternal life in heaven, and we should use every moment for His glory and honor!

In Revelation 4:11, John wrote of seeing twenty-four elders come before the throne of God, laying down their crowns, worshiping Him, and saying, "Thou art worthy, O Lord, to receive glory and honour and power: for thou hast created all things, and for thy pleasure they are and were created." Our Lord is truly worthy of all praise! There are 7.4 billion people in the world today, and just think about how much He's done in your own life and multiply that by 7.4 billion, and yet He has done even more than that! He is so wonderful and so merciful, and we often forget to thank Him for all He's done in our lives!

He is so gracious, and we are so selfish. He willingly chose to die in our place, He blesses us every day, and yet we are upset about what He didn't give us, but so many times He blesses us anyway. We can't even spare a few minutes of our day to say "Thank you, Jesus" and humbly remember how unworthy we are of His grace!

This world is so wicked—people stealing from each other, murder being such a common tragedy, people using each other to get what they want, lying, and cheating. Every day there are so many people rejecting, mocking, and displeasing the Lord. And even some

Christians are caught up in the cares of this world. Their goal is to get all the money in the world, because they think it will make them happy, but it won't. The Bible assures us that no one can buy their way into heaven, and when God destroys everything on the face of this earth, not one penny that people have claimed will remain! God will completely change the world we know and start fresh when He rules and reigns on the new earth!

God's mercy is so great that Lamentations 3:22 says, "It is of the Lord's mercies that we are not consumed, because his compassions fail not."

We need to set our eyes on the Lord of heaven and earth. Our life goal should be living to please our Creator. May we live each day for His glory and His honor, instead of our own.

2 Peter 3:18; Revelation 4:11; Psalm 147; Psalm 36:5

No Greater Love

As our Heavenly Father, God wants us to tell Him everything that's in our hearts. Even though He already knows it all, He still wants us to come before Him with an open heart, laying all our thoughts, cares, fears, sins, and worries at His feet. Jesus wants to mend our broken heart, but we must give Him all the pieces without holding back. Matthew 11:28–30 says, "Come unto me, all ye that labour and are heavy laden, and I will give you rest. Take my yoke upon you, and learn of me; for I am meek and lowly in heart: and ye shall find rest unto your souls. For my yoke is easy, and my burden is light." If we never give up our chains, we'll never be free. If we don't follow the path where the Lord is leading us, we'll only get lost on the path of our own understanding. The Lord knows what's best, but if we don't trust Him and fully submit to Him, we choose to follow the path of sin. And as the saying goes, "Sin will take you farther than you ever wanted to go!"

Nevertheless, don't ever think that you're too lost to be saved! You can always come home to Jesus asking for His forgiveness. No matter where you are, who you are, or what you've done, God's mercy will never fail. But you have to turn to Him, surrendering your life to Him. There is a huge difference between nothing and everything, which is why there is such a great change when a person receives Jesus into their life. We are nothing on our own, but it is only when Jesus steps in when we become something and we have everything. When we are weak, He makes us strong. When we are lost, He leads us home. When it seems as if we had no hope, He gives us hope.

The Lord God is so much more than words could ever describe. He loves us so very much, He shows us grace and mercy over and over again, and we constantly reject Him! He blesses us every day even though we may not see it, and yet we complain about everything. He willingly sacrificed His life to pay for what we did, and we hold back our tithes from the One Who gave us all that we have in the first place, because we're afraid He can't provide for our needs. We all need to come humbly before Him, begging for forgiveness, confessing with our whole heart that not only do we need His salvation but we need His daily help and strength.

God loves you so much, and just like a good father, He wants us to come to Him out of our own free will. He's waiting for you with arms wide open.

The Right Balance

The Bible says in Philippians 2:3, "Let each esteem other better than themselves."

Some people think that if they take something from the Bible, to the extreme, and follow that extreme through in their life, they're better than everybody else. Other people think that we should have no self-esteem and that we should consider ourselves like junk and that we have no value whatsoever, so we should live like junk.

Neither of these responses is what God is trying to tell us to do. God wants us to understand what balance is and how to live with balance. He doesn't want us to work ourselves to death, but He also doesn't want us to be lazy, but rather He wants us to have a balanced work life and use both our down time and our work time to please Him.

The Bible also says that we are of more value than many sparrows, and we see throughout the Bible that God values the sparrows because He watches them, so we know we are valued in God's eyes. Just because we are valued doesn't mean we are valued because of who we are. We must realize that our value is found in Christ, and He loves us because of His mercy and compassion toward us, insomuch that He has made a way so that we can be at peace with God!

Romans 3:10 says that there is none righteous, no, not one. This means that not you or me or anyone is counted righteous by what we can do. The only way that we are ever considered to be righteous is because when we got saved, the Lord Jesus Christ imputed His righteousness to us! Not one of us, by our own works, is perfect. And yet, so many of us think that if we follow the Old Testament law, we're better than those living under grace! This idea could not be farther from the truth! God's Word says, "For by grace are ye saved through faith; and that not of yourselves: it is the gift of God: Not of works, lest any man should boast" (Ephesians 2:8–9). God meant what He said!

Every word in the Bible, and every punctuation mark, is true. And it is from God! Not all the Scripture is written to us, but we can still learn from it, which is why God preserved it!

In God's Word, we see simple life principles, we find out more about God, and we learn how God has ordained His plan for us in this time period!

In 2 Timothy 2:15, we are told to rightly divide the word of truth, so may we rightly divide His Word, applying it where it needs to be applied in the right way it needs to be applied! God knows our hearts, and He can help us understand His Word if only we'll ask Him to show us.

God wants us to live with balance, not extremes. But in everything we do, may we do it all to the glory of God!

Numbering Our Days

Every day that goes by brings us one day closer to eternity. We really don't know what tomorrow brings. Jesus could come back in a few minutes for all we know, because when He's ready, the Lord waits for no man. We need to be ready to stand before God at any given moment! I know of so many people who are saved but live like they have fifty years until they have to stand before God, and that may or may not be true. But we need to live like today is the last day we have to run our race of faith, and we should be thankful to God every morning we wake up, for another chance we don't deserve. Within one week, I knew of two babies that were born, but I also heard that one of our friends might not be able to live much longer. In the same week, we saw God's protection in a friend's car accident. We never know what the day is going to hold, so we need to be prepared for anything to happen. This does not mean we should be so careful that we worry ourselves to death about what could happen. But before we do anything, we need to ask ourselves, "Is this pleasing to God? Can He bless what I'm doing with my life?"

Many times, we take our religious freedom for granted. On Sunday morning, we stay in bed because it feels nice and cozy, instead of getting up and going to church. When we should be doing our daily devotions, we're watching television, playing a game, or sleeping in some more. I'm as guilty of it as anyone else is, and I'm ashamed of it. But I know that if we'd all do what's pleasing to the Lord rather than what's pleasing to ourselves, we would have a much better life. Because so many of us have eliminated the reading of God's Word from our everyday lives, we have let the devil control parts of our lives, such as the music we listen to, the people we spend time with, what comes out of our mouths, and what consumes our time. The Bible talks about everything involved in life and in death. We will all face death at some time in our lives, but are we all ready for death today? We should be, because this life we have been given and it is not ours to decide when it ends, but God did give us the chance to choose where we spend eternity.

There's a song where the chorus goes like this: "Jesus, oh Jesus! Do you know Him today? Please don't turn Him away. Oh Jesus, oh Jesus! Without Him, how lost I would be!"

I'd like to encourage you to take a moment to think about what your life would be like right now if you were still lost in sin and then take a minute to praise God for His mercy and grace in your life! He deserves to hear so much more than a simple "Dear God, thank You for this food. Amen," but He deserves our hearts.

We don't know what today has in store for us. We could die in an instant, so we need to be ready to face eternity today, and we should be urged to do something more for God while we still have this moment to live with the chance to tell the world what Jesus has done for us!

May we use every breath the Lord has so graciously given us for His glory and honor!

Psalm 90:12 says, "So teach us to number our days, that we may apply our hearts unto wisdom."

Hebrews 13:4; Psalm 9:8; Psalm 96:13; John 7:24; Revelation 20:11–13

Moving Mountains

M atthew 17:20 says, "And Jesus said unto them, Because of your unbelief: for verily I say unto you, If ye have faith as a grain of mustard seed, ye shall say unto this mountain, Remove hence to yonder place; and it shall remove; and nothing shall be impossible unto you."

I recently heard a story of a woman who lived among some mountains, and she didn't have much sunshine in her home. She heard that if she had faith the size of a mustard seed, she could speak to that mountain and it would move. One day, she said, "God, move that mountain!" And when she woke up the next morning, the mountain was still there, and she said, "Just as I expected!"

So many times we sell God short, and we think that all God's ever done is in the past and that He's not able to move mountains and part waters anymore. Let me be the first to tell you that God is still a mountain-moving God and if He wanted to, He could part the Pacific Ocean (the deepest body of water) in two! Some of us are separated from our loved ones, and it hurts I know, but I believe with all my heart that God will move those mountains of separation and we will see each other face-to-face instead of through a video chat when we all get to heaven!

If we don't believe that God can, we don't believe that He will, because He wants to see us operate in belief and He wants us to have faith that He is still the God of the impossible!

Just like it says in Hebrews 11:1, "Now faith is the substance of things hoped for, the evidence of things not seen." When we have faith that God can move the mountain blocking our sunlight, we don't see how God can do it, but we simply believe that He will.

If we would live our lives in belief as often as we live in unbelief, we would have so much more sunshine in our homes and in our everyday lives! We need to pray expecting God to answer. We need to tithe trusting God will provide. There are so many things that we can do to put our faith into action. The question is, When will we start!?

God created all that is, He owns the cattle on a thousand hills, and surely He is able to do far more than we could ever imagine. So may we live our lives operating in belief, watching God move mountains and part waters, seeing Him provide every need, and experiencing the sunshine and the joy that we have as Christians!

Matthew 13:58; Hebrews 11:6; Mark 11:22–23; Psalm 46:1–3; Isaiah 40:28–31; Matthew 19:26; Proverbs 20:6

Once Saved, Always Saved

Some people believe that if you turn away from God, He'll turn away from you, but I don't believe that at all. I believe that what the Bible says is true and what God promises, He fulfills and there's absolutely no one that can overthrow our Lord! The Bible says in Ephesians 1:13, "Ye were sealed with that holy Spirit of promise," and I know that my God is a God Who keeps His promises!

I've witnessed this verse put into action! I gave my life to Jesus when I was five, but I didn't start living like I was saved until I was thirteen. I tried to find true, lasting love in other people but didn't find it. I searched for happiness in things that couldn't give me joy, and I searched for peace in music that wasn't even peaceful! Yet, God was faithful, and His spirit did not keep silent inside me. And even after all I had done, He still forgave me. Not one day after the day I trusted Christ as my personal Savior when I was five years old did God ever leave me alone! For that, I am so thankful. And now that God has worked in my heart to show me that His love was what I was looking for and I didn't even realize that I was already loved with the most genuine and everlasting love, I am the happiest person today! I did not find my joy, peace, love, and self-acceptance in the things I chased after. But I found it all in Jesus, and I have all I'll ever need!

Jesus saved me on November 23, 2009, not because of what I could do. But He saved me because of what He already did on the cross of Calvary! When I couldn't pay my sin debt, Jesus stepped up and paid it for me! If God could save me and if He could save the demon-possessed man in Mark 5 and everybody else whom He's already saved, I guarantee you He can save you! He's never met one person whom He can't save, and He's not going to start today! No matter how lost in sin you may be, you're never too lost to be saved. But one day it will be too late, and you'll be wishing for one more chance.

For those of us who are saved, we need to live more like it, not because if we don't we'll lose our salvation. But we should live for the Lord because every breath we have is a gift from Him and everything we have is an example of His great mercy, and we should want to please Him with our lives! Some people think that you can lose your salvation, but I have done a lot of reading and praying, and what I've learned is this: the Bible is true because God preserved it so that we can learn from it and can know the truth (Psalm 119:160; John 8:32).

Once we're sealed with that Holy Spirit, we can't unseal ourselves (Ephesians 1:13; John 10:28–29).

We have the only true and lasting hope in Jesus Christ, because He's alive! Mohammed is still in the grave, Buddha is still in the grave, and all the other "little g" gods are still in the grave. But we as Christians can put our faith and trust in the Lord Jesus Christ because He's *not* dead. *He's alive!* (1 Corinthians 15:18–20).

We serve a risen Savior, and so many times, we don't live like it at all, but we can rejoice always because the Giver of all joy is our Redeemer and He loves us!

My thoughts are if God won't forgive us when we turn away from Him to run back to sin, why would He have forgiven us when we were dead in sin before He saved us (Ephesians 2:1–5)? Our God is merciful, and He shows His love toward us every day whether we realize it or not, and His faithfulness is greater than we can ever know.

If there is anyone who has not trusted Jesus as their personal Savior, I want to tell you *today is the day of salvation*, for the Lord could come back the very next moment and the next time you blink your eyes, it may be too late! Don't wait.

Come to Jesus. He will not fail you!

Romans 5:8; Romans 5:20; Titus 3:5; Ephesians 2:8–9; Psalm 89:33

Into His Hands

Entrusting someone who is so special to us into God's hands is hard, but we have no reason to hold back. Jesus gave us everything, and yet we can't bring ourselves to let go of the ones we hold so close to our hearts. He's the One Who placed them in our lives in the first place. And He is their Creator, Redeemer, and Lord! I understand how hard it is to trust God to protect someone whom we've buried so deep in our hearts, but the truth is we need to entrust our loved ones into the hands of the true and living God. They're so much safer in God's all-powerful hands than in our own hands. So many times, we hold tight to our loved ones, and that's good that we love and care for them. But when Jesus asks us to trust Him with their life and we refuse to, that is not good at all. We have so many reasons to trust the Lord, but yet, we often don't!

Jeremiah 32:17–27 says a lot, but the beginning and end is my favorite part, "Ah Lord God! behold, thou hast made the heaven and the earth by thy great power and stretched out arm, and there is nothing too hard for thee: Then came the word of the Lord unto Jeremiah, saying, Behold, I am the Lord, the God of all flesh: is there any thing too hard for me?"

Wow! These are only a few reasons we can trust our God! He's not only able to protect our loved ones, but He's able to give them so much more than we could ever give them. So may we trust the God of all flesh and entrust to Him all our cares and our worries! He is worthy of our praise and our trust, and may we trust Him more and more every single day!

Psalm 5:3; Ephesians 3:20; Exodus 33:14

Somebody Cares about You

One day, while on the way to language school, I saw a man, with gray hair, a gray hat, and torn clothing. And he was pulling a small bag with wheels. He was obviously homeless. He looked at me as we drove by, and I saw his eyes were filled with tears. We were driving by so fast, and all I could think of was how much hurt he was feeling and how much joy he could be feeling through Jesus Christ. It made me so sad, but it also reminded me of God's burden on my heart to reach the homeless people with God's love. I had been so down that week, just missing home, and I had forgotten that God had big plans for my life. And even though I may not understand why He's having me sit still right now and making me wait so long, I know that He is teaching me things along the way, and I need to be learning from what He does in my life today.

So many people I know are going through health problems, and though we do not understand why they're stuck in a hospital bed or having to go through multiple treatments for a small chance to live, we can put our faith and trust in the Great Physician, Who is able to heal them if it be His will.

When we're going through a trial, we feel weak. But somehow, by the grace of God, we always come out stronger than we were before! All of us can find something to be grateful for every day, no matter what we're going through!

Never give up! God is working, and He is fulfilling His marvelous plan for your life, even today!

No matter how discouraged we may be, we can look to Jesus in times of trouble, trusting that He will bring us through. And we can rest in the fact that He cares for us. He loved us enough to die on the cross for our sins, and He loves us for what He did, not for what we can do. May we share the joy of Jesus Christ to those around us, and may we shine the light that we have through Him to this dark, lost, and dying world.

2 Corinthians 5:21; James 1:12; Matthew 5:6; Matthew 5:10–14; Romans 12:1–2

Come Home

Like most missionaries on the field, I was always counting down the days to the day we'd fly home for the holidays! We love to be home with the ones we love, but there are some people who don't want to go home, and I'm not just talking about our physical home but also about our spiritual home. As Christians, we are God's children, and our home is in heaven with Him.

So many times, we get attached to this world, and we forget that we're just traveling through.

The devil likes to use the things of this world to distract us from focusing on living our life for Jesus Christ.

In Luke 15:11–32 it talks about the parable of the prodigal son. We are sometimes like the prodigal son. We think that we can do things better than our Heavenly Father can, so we set out on our own, and the devil deceives us to walk the paths of pride. We then suffer the consequences of our sins and realize how foolish we've been. We then run back home, and much to our surprise, we find that our Father was longing for us to come home and live in the blessings He has for us! We admit that we're wrong, and because our God is so rich in mercy, He forgives us and calls for a celebration to welcome us back home!

Sadly, not all of us have come back home yet, but it's not too late! Your Heavenly Father is longing for you to come home! The first step is always the hardest, but there will be great rejoicing when you come home!

For those of you who aren't saved, you'll never be too lost to be saved, but time is running out! You may wake up tomorrow morning and find out that the rapture happened last night. Thoughts rush through your mind, and you remember what your response was when people asked you to get saved. "Tomorrow," you said, and only now do you realize tomorrow was too late. Don't wait until tomorrow; it may be too late. Come home while you still can. Jesus is longing for you to come home to Him!

Lamentations 3:22; Luke 15:10; Psalm 86:5; Proverbs 28:13; 1 John 2:2

Befriending the Right Enemy

In Matthew 5:43–44, Jesus says, "Ye have heard that it hath been said, Thou shalt love thy neighbor, and hate thine enemy. But I say unto you, Love your enemies, bless them that curse you, do good to them that hate you, and pray for them which despitefully use you, and persecute you." We hear this verse quite often, but we hardly ever put it into practice. Don't you think that if Jesus commanded us to do something, we ought to jump right up and do it? We all have people in our lives who have hurt us, and we usually consider them our enemies, but it's very important to remember that God loves them just as much as He loves us. And as hard as it is to let go of the grudge we've been holding on to, we need to forgive them like Jesus forgave them and us. I know it's hard, and we won't love them overnight. But if we ask God to help us love them, He will.

God wants us to love our enemies. There is only one enemy He doesn't want us to befriend, and that is the devil. Jesus said in John 10:10, "The thief cometh not, but for to steal, and to kill, and to destroy: I am come that they might have life, and that they might have it more abundantly." Satan has deceived so many people by making them think that he's their friend, that he can be trusted, and that he doesn't want us to miss out on the best times of our lives. But we're warned about this enemy and told to resist him in James 4:7. Satan cannot be trusted, and he only wants to turn your trust away from God. The devil doesn't care about you, and as soon as you reap the consequences of your actions, you will no longer be partying with the devil. The expense of sin is never worth it, but Jesus paid it all, and you can be forgiven if you turn to Him!

May we love God above all else, and with His help may we love and pray for our "enemies" and resist the real enemy—the devil!

Romans 12:8; John 13:34; 2 Peter 3:9; 1 Peter 5:8

The True Hero

Today we celebrate the sacrifice of many warriors who gave their lives for our freedom. They knew what true sacrifice was, and they made no hesitation when called upon to make it.

Sacrifice has been all throughout history—from the shedding of blood from animals in the Old Testament to the shedding of the innocent blood of Jesus Christ in our place and then all the shed blood of men and women we call "heroes."

The word *hero* is defined as "a person who is admired or idealized for courage, outstanding achievements, or noble qualities."

If we think about those deep and pure attributes in such a person, we discover that the greatest hero of all time is Jesus Christ! The humility and courage He had, to be crucified for our very own sins, ought to humble us and cause us to courageously thank Him for His great sacrifice for us!

You see, we cannot be truly grateful to anyone else until we are truly grateful to Christ for saving us! The very best example of what a sacrifice should be like is the one laid down by our Savior!

The Bible says we are to die daily (1 Corinthians 15:31). Are we? Are we dying daily to our fleshly desires, motives, and habits? Or are we neglecting the sacrifice God wants us to make? Remember God will never ask you to do more for Him than He has done for you!

You can never top God in giving, but when you give with the right heart, it pleases Him greatly!

I feel like sometimes we pay more attention to the sacrifices made by ordinary people than we do the great sacrifice made by our great God! We should always put God before man—always. No matter how strange that makes the world look at us or how many criticizing remarks we get, we should always want to sacrifice our daily hearts and lives to the Lord Jesus Christ, Who gave everything to us!

Today we also celebrate the men and women who died serving our country, and it's comforting to the families. But we have every reason to give thanks to the Lord Who rose from that sad and ugly grave and is right now set down at the right hand of God the Father! He's alive!

He gave us the ultimate sacrifice, and we have the opportunity to come before His presence and worship Him for what He's done! We don't have to wait till we get to heaven to worship Him. We ought to start warming up to that hallelujah party right now!

If there was ever a time when you were sinking down in sin and had no hope or joy within but then you called on Jesus and asked Him to save you, you and I have every reason to call out to Him today and thank Him! Thank Him for what He's given you—a home in heaven, a hope and a joy that cannot be explained, and a peace that cannot be understood! Somebody praise the Lord today, for His merciful sacrifice for us!

Philippians 2:5–11; Hebrews 10:19; Ephesians 3:12; John 12:43; John 15:13; Ephesians 1:6

Prepared or Preparing?

Jesus is coming soon. This thrills my soul but also urges me to be more of a witness to those around me. Paul said in Philippians 1:23–24, "For I am in a strait betwixt two, having a desire to depart, and to be with Christ; which is far better: Nevertheless to abide in the flesh is more needful for you." God has us where we are today for a reason. Maybe it's to lead a soul to Christ, maybe it's to encourage someone, or maybe it's to increase your own faith. But even when we don't know why things happen the way they do, we can trust God to bring us through all the problems of life. And we can look forward to eternity in heaven, where everything will be glorious, forever.

Mark 13:32 says, "But of that day and that hour knoweth no man, no, not the angels which are in heaven, neither the Son, but the Father."

Jesus could come to get His children at any given moment, and we should be prepared, not still preparing. Just like in the game of hide-and-seek, once the seeker is done counting, he says, "Ready or not, here I come!" We all need to be ready to stand before God, because He comes quickly and He comes on His own time (Revelation 22:12)!

Are you ready to see Jesus face-to-face? I certainly hope so because tomorrow may be too late.

1 Corinthians 15:52; Mark 13:32; 2 Corinthians 5:10; Acts 1:7

Rags to Riches

*W*e can always do something more for Jesus. We can never give Him more than He has given us, which is why our salvation cannot be earned but received. It is a free unmerited gift, and all we have to do is receive it. Even once we get saved, our righteousness is still as filthy rags. The only righteousness we have as Christians is God's.

So many times, people get mad at God when something bad happens, but why is it when something good happens, we forget about God and take the credit for ourselves when it really belongs to God? Jesus did *not* owe us anything! The only thing we deserved was hell, yet Jesus chose to love us and to willingly lay down His life for us, and then He rose from the grave! Most of the time when something bad happens in our lives, God is trying to teach us something. But if we aren't willing to learn, we make the trial even harder by not listening and allowing the Potter to form us into what He wants us to be.

So many times, we leave God the leftovers of our everyday lives, but we wouldn't be able to live if He hadn't given His life for us.

If I was to ask you what your main priority in life is, what would you say? Now, what if God was to ask you what your main priority in life was? My guess is it would be two totally different answers. Did you know that the word *priority* wasn't pluralized until the 1940s?

This could be because God only intended for man to have one single priority—Himself.

Life gets busy, but our number one priority should be Jesus Christ and fulfilling His will for our life. So from this day forward, may we strive to live for God and not for ourselves. And may we never forget what Jesus has done, is doing, and will do for us. He gave it all. What are we giving to Him?

Isaiah 64:6; Colossians 3:2; Matthew 6:19–21; Matthew 6:24; Matthew 6:33; Isaiah 6:23

Love That Cost a Cross

Valentine's Day is the day we find ways to tell our loved ones that we love them, and that's great, but maybe this year we can do something to tell Jesus that we love Him.

We all enjoy it when someone tells us that they love us, and so does Jesus. He set the ultimate example of what love really is, and we forget to thank Him for His gift of love to us.

Valentine's Day is a day to celebrate our love for one another, and we often show everyone how much we love them, except Jesus Christ. We need to let our Savior know how much we love and appreciate Him and how our life would be nothing without Him!

He loved us so much more than we can ever understand. Philippians 2:5–8 says,

> Let this mind be in you, which was also in Christ Jesus: Who, being in the form of God, thought it not robbery to be equal with God: But made himself of no reputation, and took upon him the form of a servant, and was made in the likeness of men: And being found in fashion as a man, he humbled himself, and became obedient unto death, even the death of the cross.

Jesus Christ took our punishment for sin, and He loved us so much that He left His throne in glory and gave up everything, so that we could be saved.

In all history, there was no love greater than Jesus's love for us, and there will never be so great a love in time to come. But how much do we love Him? How evident is our love for Him?

Christ loved us so much, but if He hadn't put it into action, we would've never known.

We can love someone so much and never say anything about it, and it won't change a thing.

On the other hand, we can love someone so much and put it into action, and it could change everything!

This Valentine's Day may we take the time to write a love letter to the One Who loved us first and paid our debt on Calvary's tree and Who still loves us with an undying, unending love!

But may we not just put our love into words on a sheet of paper, but may we put it into action in our everyday lives.

John 15:13; Isaiah 53:3–7; John 3:16; Hebrews 12:2

Pray Believing

Psalm 18:6 says, "In my distress I called upon the Lord, and cried unto my God: he heard my voice out of his temple, and my cry came before him, even into his ears."

When we pray, we should pray believing that God will answer. The answer will not always be yes. Sometimes He says no for our good, and sometimes (a lot of times) God says wait. One of the times God said wait was in John 11:1–45, when Lazarus was dying and the answer was wait, so that God could be glorified when Lazarus walked out of the grave. At first, Martha didn't understand why Jesus didn't rush there to heal him, but she didn't have to understand. She just needed to believe that Jesus knew best and that He could do the unexpected. She believed. And because of their faith, her brother was resurrected from the dead, and the Lord was magnified.

That just goes to show how faithful our God is! He hears our prayers, and He *will* answer! Sometimes He cries with us first, instead of getting right to the point. He shares our grief, and He is our ever-present friend and comfort in the good times and bad times!

We need to remember to not only run to God for the answers when problems come, but we need to be running to God every day. Even a simple "Thank You, Lord" throughout the day puts a smile on God's face and reminds us to be grateful for what He's so graciously given us. Even though He already knows our needs, He wants to hear from us, just like a father wants to hear from his child. We are also told that in Hebrews 4:16 that we can come to the throne of God with boldness and confidence!

When we ask for something, we should pray, expecting Him to answer, and trust that He knows what's best.

Psalm 94:9; Psalm 19:3; Psalm 34:6; Psalm 55:17; Isaiah 65:24; Matthew 6:8; Matthew 7:7; Matthew 17:20; Luke 1:37; 1 Thessalonians 5:17; Hebrews 11:6; Ephesians 6:18

By God's Strength

God has a specific calling on the life of each one of us.

Some of us are fulfilling that calling, while others may not even know what God's specifically calling them to do yet.

No matter what, we must always remember to do all our work not only for God but by God!

We need to do everything in the strength and guidance of the Lord!

The Bible says for us to do all to the glory of God, but how can we give God glory in the little things, such as cleaning or cooking or simply showing up for work each day?

I believe that by recognizing that it is not by our strength that we can do things but it is only by God's strength that we can do anything!

If God calls us to do something, no matter how big or how small, we need to remember that the same God Who called us is the same God Who will give us the strength to do it!

Recently, God has opened my eyes to the fact that Philippians 4:13 is misinterpreted too many times. It says, "I can do all things through Christ which strengtheneth me."

We often think this means that we can do all things because Christ gives us the strength, but the context of the word *which* suggests a different meaning. But rather, it means that the fact that I can do all things through Christ strengthens me!

We can do all things through Christ, not because of our own strength but because of His strength! The statement made in Philippians 4:13 is very encouraging, and therefore it increases our trust and reliance on Christ!

By giving the glory to whom it belongs, we are made to be a channel of God's grace, and we can see in a more genuine way the power and strength of God!

2 Chronicles 16:9

Changing the World

It's not my job to change the world. That's God's job if it be His will, and we know that it is His will, because it's His will that all should come to repentance!

One soul at a time, this world can be changed by the working of the Holy Spirit in the heart of every born-again believer. When we as Christians do the right thing, the part of the world that needed to change is being transformed day by day. So as we let God change the world, rather than taking this humanly impossible task on our own shoulders, we must let the change we want to see around us start in the hearts of God's children!

When I think of the changes I'd like to see in the world around me, I think of what could support this surrounding change, that is, if I myself would let the Holy Spirit change my motives and actions to be after His will and heart.

I want the world to be more grateful. Then, first, I must be more grateful!

I want the world to be less arrogant. Then, first, I must be selfless.

I want the world to be without cussing and profanity. Then, first, I must not use cussing and profanity.

I want the world to be more Christlike. Then, first, I must be more Christlike.

I want the world to know Christ as their personal Savior and Friend. Then, first, I must know Christ as my personal Savior and Friend and let His light shine through me for His glory and purpose.

Let each change you want to see in others begin within your own self, and with time and perseverance, you will start to see fruit. Always remember seeds must first be planted, then be watered, then have sunshine, and have time to grow.

How will you let God change you today?

Focus

With my hometown being so close to Lancaster, Pennsylvania, I have seen a lot of Amish people riding their horses and buggies on the road. When a horse is on the road, he has blinders on so that he doesn't get spooked by the cars. Just like the horse, we need to put our blinders on throughout our everyday life. The cars are our problems and worries, and we need to focus on God, the One Who can solve our problems. The minute we move our eyes off Him, we become scared and anxious by focusing on our problems, instead of keeping our focus on the Lord.

Like Peter when he was walking on the water with Jesus, the minute he looked at the storm was the very same moment he began to sink (Matthew 14:22–33). Peter cried out to the Lord, and *immediately* He stretched out His hand to save him.

There's no place that God cannot hear you, but you must call out to Him first (Jonah 2:2).

As soon as you call out for Him to save you, He will reach out immediately and save you!

Think of when you're taking a picture. It makes the world of difference when the camera is focused on the *right* subject.

We read in Luke 10:38–42 how Martha was worried about the things around the house, trying to please Jesus with material things, but Mary pleased Jesus by focusing on Him and listening to what He had to say.

Many times, the reason God tells us to focus on Him, and not our circumstances, is for our own good. He's trying to teach us something through that storm. But if we don't pay attention to the teacher, we won't learn anything, and most likely, we'll have to take the test again.

When we focus on God, we have no time to worry and no reason to fear. So may we live our lives focusing on the right subject, and may we live every day God's given us with Jesus as our focal point.

Hebrews 12:1–3; Colossians 3:2; Isaiah 41:10; Proverbs 4:25

Nothing but the Blood

John 14:6 says, "Jesus saith unto him, I am the way, the truth, and the life: no man cometh unto the Father, but by me."

People are always trying to find another way to get to heaven other than the only true way, which is Jesus Christ! There are 4,200 religions in the world today, and the truth is not one of them can give you eternal life.

Every religion has at least one ritual that they practice, thinking that it will either bring them good luck, keep away evil spirits, cover their sins, or even get them to heaven.

Catholics pray to Mary, believing that she is the mediator between God and man. But the Bible clearly says in 1 Timothy 2:5, "For there is one God, and one mediator between God and men, the man Christ Jesus." So when people pray to Mary, what they are really doing is making her an idol. She needed a Savior just as much as we do, and she admitted that in Luke 1:47.

That just goes to show how easy it is to make anything in our life an idol. We need to be careful that we keep the *one true living God* the only One Whom we serve and worship.

So many people profess to be a Christian, but a Christian is not someone who professes Christ but rather someone who *possesses* Christ as their Lord and Savior. The only way that a person can get saved is if he realizes he is a sinner, needs a Savior, and calls out to God asking Him to save him. I believe that it is in that very moment that the Holy Spirit comes into that person's heart and that soul is sealed unto the day of redemption. Nothing that we could ever do can save us from our sins, which is why when we get saved, God imputes His righteousness to us. We will never be perfect. Only God was, is, and forever will be.

Religion will not save you. Jesus's blood that was shed on the cross is the only way that we can have eternal life. Anything else, and it's hell forever.

Trust Him *today* if you haven't already, and I promise you, you will never regret it!

Isaiah 43:11; Ephesians 4:30; 1 Peter 1:19; 2 Corinthians 5:21; Galatians 3:13

The Past Is Forgiven

Some people come up with the crazy idea that they're too broken to be fixed or, in other words, too lost to be saved. Nothing could be farther from the truth!

Luke 19:10 states, "For the Son of man is come to seek and to save that which was lost."

If Jesus didn't come to save *sinners*, then whom did He come to save? Healthy people don't need a doctor; sick people do! Jesus came for us, because we need Him!

Romans 3:23 says, "For all have sinned, and come short of the glory of God."

There isn't one person on this earth who has never sinned. Without Jesus Christ, we are *all lost* and on our way to hell, but the good news is there is hope! Jesus came to save that which was *lost*! You only have to put your trust in Him and confess that you are nothing on your own, and He *will* save you!

We all have a past, but when we get saved, Jesus buries our past and has forgiven us of our sins—past, present, and future!

Many times, after you get saved, the devil's greatest weapon is your past. He brings it up in your path as a stumbling block, to get you to question your salvation, to distract you from running the Christian race, or to lure you back into the temptation of sin.

When that happens, you need to jump right over that obstacle and remind him that it is no longer remembered by your Lord and Savior. And you can keep on living for Jesus, the One Who buried your past and covered it with His blood! Don't let the devil haunt you with a debt that's already been paid! Jesus buried my past, and no matter how hard the devil tries to dig it up, he can't!

Maybe the reason Satan is trying to distract you is because he sees a soul on the road ahead that you could lead to the Lord. Or maybe there's a trial coming, and if he can come between you and your Savior, you'll be most miserable while going through it. We'll never know what's ahead, but we'll never find out if we don't stop focusing on the past.

We can run ahead without fear, when we're walking hand in hand with the Lord, because He is the only One Who can help us through the journey. In order for God to open a door to your future, you have to let go of the past.

It was said in a sermon, "We can't know someone in the present if we don't stop looking at the past." This is so true!

It's so simple to be saved, but it's difficult to run the Christian race, simply because Satan is always trying to stop us. But we must keep on, and we must not give in to the devil's lies.

With Jesus as our guide, we can keep running the race! I'm not saying it's easy. It most certainly is not easy, but it's absolutely worth it.

The hymn "When We See Christ" greatly explains when it will be worth all the perseverance we should have until that day!

> It will be worth it all when we see Jesus,
> Life's trials will seem so small when we see Christ;
> One glimpse of His dear face all sorrow will erase,
> So bravely run the race till we see Christ."

So let's bravely run the race and not let our past keep us from the joy that is set before us!

Psalm 51:3; Hebrews 12:1–3; Ephesians 2:13; Philippians 3:14; 1 John 1:9; Ephesians 4:32; James 4:7; Proverbs 1:10

Watching for the King

Every morning the sun comes up, we could be entering our last day. Jesus could come back at any moment, and when Jesus is ready to come back for His redeemed, there's nothing that's gonna stop or hinder His appearance!

The Bible says in Matthew 24:42–44 that we need to be prepared at all times, because we do not know when Jesus is coming back.

Sadly, so many of us overlook the fact that it could be today! We often think that we have more time, but we don't know that for sure. The truth is it's not our job to know when He's coming back, but our job is to be ready and to be a faithful witness until that day! When we get to heaven, we want to hear the Father tell us, "Well done, my good and faithful servant!" But He isn't going to say that if it isn't true.

We need to be strong and courageous no matter how hard our struggles pull us down. We need to remember that when we fall off the horse, we need to get right back on.

Many times, missionaries leave the field because the language was too hard to learn, the people were not very friendly, or they miss the comforts of home too much. I agree with all my heart it is hard, but I believe the devil is always trying to pull us down in some way or another, but it's those times especially when we must remain strong and seek God's face and strength every day!

All throughout the book of Psalms, David called the Lord his high tower, his strong refuge, and his rock. This is a great reminder that the Lord is a firm foundation that will never change and He will protect us from the enemies when we run to Him for safety. God placed each one of us where we are for His divine purpose.

It's never easy to get back on the horse, but it's worth it! There could be a lost soul waiting for you to share the gospel with them or someone who needs encouraged to keep living for Christ.

Every day, we are a witness and a testimony to our children, our spouse, our coworkers, and everyone around us! They will either see someone who is living for themselves or for the Lord.

Many times, we get so focused on meeting our material needs that we don't focus on spiritual needs, but Jesus is the only One Who provides us with what we have. We are only stewards of His gifts, which is why we need to not live for earthly riches but rather for heavenly crowns, which we will ultimately cast at Jesus's feet. Money has *no* eternal value whatsoever, nor does a high place in society. A soul that will face eternity, that's what has true eternal value to God. He wants us to focus on serving Him and let Him put the rest of the puzzle pieces into place! Physical things may change our lives temporarily, but spiritual things will change our lives for an eternity!

We need to have a passion for lost souls, not the things of this world! So may we keep living for our Redeemer and King and remember that it could be today that He returns!

2 Corinthians 4:3–4; Psalm 62:7; 1 Corinthians 15:52; 1 Corinthians 15:58; Matthew 5:16

Freedom Taken for Granted

As Americans, we have so many privileges that we take for granted. We have freedom to worship God and go to church, yet so many of us sleep in rather than go to church. There are over two thousand languages that do not have God's written Word in their language, and yet we have the Word of God in English, and how many times do we leave it sitting on a shelf instead of reading it!? Some people can't even read, and we have the education they don't, and we would rather read books of fiction than the true and preserved Bible that some are longing to read. We have cupboards full of food at our fingertips, while others are starving. God has blessed America through the years because of the good Christian leaders our country had, who made sure that God was magnified in all they did. Look at our money and the pledge of allegiance, and at the end of our national anthem, it says, "And this be our motto—In God is our trust." America is so blessed because God blessed it! May we remember the reason America is so great is because our God is so great! Psalm 33:12; Psalm 20:7; Matthew 6:33

We Sorrow Not

The first letter of Paul to the Thessalonians 4:13–14 says, "But I would not have you to be ignorant, brethren, concerning them which are asleep, that ye sorrow not, even as others which have no hope. For if we believe that Jesus died and rose again, even so them also which sleep in Jesus will God bring with him." With the recent passing of my one-hundred-year-old great-grandma, I would say this verse is a great comfort to me. We don't have to sorrow for a long period of time like the rest of this world does, because we know that she was saved and that she is in heaven right now, with the One Who died for her sins and for our sins. She's with her husband, and she is no longer in pain. We can rejoice in the fact that we have hope! We who have been saved by God's grace will see her again, and we'll never say "goodbye" again!

As a missionary, the most used word in my life is *goodbye*. The most comforting thing to me about heaven is knowing that there's coming a day when I will never say goodbye again and I will forever be with most of my loved ones, in a place where we'll never get sick and die and, together, we will worship the Lord for all eternity! As a Christian, I have hope!

Tomorrow is an unsure thing, and the past is a sure thing that I cannot change. Right here in this moment, I am living under grace. And I can rejoice in the fact that Jesus loves me, died for me, rose again, and is living in my heart today and forever. And it's all by His amazing grace!

When Jesus saved me, He didn't save me under a contract, where I have to do so many things to earn my salvation. No, salvation is a free, unmerited gift that anyone can receive. If we are saved by grace (which we are), then it's no longer grace if we try to earn it. The Bible tells us that today, we can accept the free gift of salvation, by grace through faith. And then in our love for the Lord, we serve Him with our every breath because it brings Him glory and pleasure!

As His children, we should want to please our Heavenly Father, just like a child should want to bring his earthly father pleasure. The truth is everyone will die one day, some sooner than others. But as Christians, if the person who died had accepted Jesus Christ as their personal Savior, we have no reason to sorrow because we're only being separated for a short period of time. And when we join them (whether it be by death or the rapture), we will be together forever. We have a living hope! Our Redeemer lives! Christians should be the happiest people on this earth, and yet why is it so many times we are the ones who complain the most?

We need to look at what we have in Christ and focus on what He's already given us! We don't deserve one thing! Everything we have is by God's grace! How many times a week do we thank Him for what He did for us on the cross of Calvary? The cross that our sins nailed Him to? It's terrible to think that most of us might only thank Him once a week, when really we are saved 24-7! How often do we praise Him for our eternal, living hope? May we remember just how blessed we are, instead of constantly complaining to God for what we don't have!

Psalm 42:11; Lamentations 3:21–25; Romans 12:11–12; Ephesians 2:12–14; Colossians 1:5; Titus 2:13

What's Your Wattage?

*I*n a world where darkness hits close to home and everything comes crashing in around us, we can remember the hope we have is not in vain. Even in the darkness, the light of Christ is still shining!

Jesus is not the light at the end of the tunnel but the light in the tunnel! We were given that light the very moment we got saved, but it's up to us to let it shine or not. In this dark world, you and I have a light. Are we letting it shine into the darkness?

The Bible says that the gospel is hid to those who are lost, until the light of the glorious gospel should shine unto them! Are we letting the light shine so that others can see it? Others are living in the same dark world we are in, but the difference is they don't have the light we do!

Lights all have different wattages. Some are brighter than others, and some are not even bright enough to notice. So my question for us all is simply this, What wattage is your light shining at today?

Is it at a low wattage so that only a few people can see it? Or is it shining brightly so that everyone around us can see the magnificent hope we have?

How can we brighten our bulb? We can strengthen our connection with the source of our light, and that is Jesus Christ! His power is infinite, and once we get in contact with Him and let Him work in our lives, we will begin to see the darkness fade away because the Light inside of us is so brightly burning!

God's Word also says that we are not to be overcome of evil, but we are to overcome evil with good. We are more than conquerors through our Lord Jesus Christ! He is the One Who gives us the victory, so why do we try to do things on our own and expect the same victory that Christ has already won? He conquered all darkness that resurrection morning. And His spirit lives inside of every born-again believer, to guide them and comfort them in this sinful world, giving every Christian the light sufficient to shine unto the hearts of the lost people all around us! If we would only stop hiding it under a bushel, then we would see how the light of Christ can transform the darkness into even more light!

How are we shining our light today? Are we living defeated by the darkness, or are we living in the victorious light Christ has given us?

2 Corinthians 4:3–4; Romans 12:21

Tradition, or Truth?

Throughout history, people have created many different traditions that have been passed on from generation to generation—for example, holiday traditions, family traditions, cultural traditions, and even religious traditions.

Very few people have passed the truth on to the next generations. Many Christians today will decide what version of the Bible to use by what everyone else is using and stick with the world's tradition rather than searching for the *truth*! God has given us His truth, but we so proudly and lazily let it sit on a shelf, praying that it will miraculously fall in our laps. But that's not how it works! If you're hungry but are too lazy to get up and walk into the kitchen to get some food, you cannot expect the food to magically appear in front of you without getting up and looking for food!

It's the exact same way with spiritual food! God gave us the most nutritious, healthy, energizing spiritual food that we need. But we are too busy with our traditions to humble ourselves and live on the Word of *truth*! Nowadays, with modern technology, we have our phone connected to our fingers all the time. We just download a Bible app and read it from a screen when we don't make time to get off our high horse and turn the physical pages of God's holy, written Word. People who aren't allowed to have a physical Bible are limited to the Bible apps, but they long for the precious physical Bible that they can hold in their hands. In America and every other free country, God has given us the freedom that our country has fought for. We ought to be humble and grateful enough to use it!

It's very irritating to see people who live the way they do because of the traditions that they've been taught! So many of the traditions are *not* biblical and not to be applied to this period of time.

2 Timothy 2:15 instructs us, "Study to shew thyself approved unto God, a workman that needeth not to be ashamed, rightly dividing the word of truth."

The truth is hard to find because this temporary, wicked earth is filled with Satan's deceiving lies that people have been fooled by, but since the truth is hard to find, it will not be the most popular on the market or the easiest-to-understand "Bible." God blesses those who search diligently and humbly for the truth, and He will give wisdom and understanding to those who ask.

People have been taught by tradition what Bible to use, what music to listen to, what gospel to preach, and what "religion" to follow. And everyone has a different opinion on these things. But do they have a solid foundation to base their beliefs, their stands, and their way of life upon? If in the end, you are standing only on God's Word of truth, then that is truly what God wants you to do! On the other hand, if what you believe is based upon what other people are doing or on what your traditions are, then it is nothing but sandy lies and thorny bushes.

So may this encourage us to search the scriptures for the truth that applies to us today, and may we daily live and breathe His *truth* for the glory of God!

Psalm 33:4; Psalm 12:6–8; Proverbs 30:5–6; 2 Timothy 2:15; Acts 16:30–31; Ephesians 2:8–9; 2 Corinthians 4:3–4; Proverbs 19:21; 2 Timothy 2:3–4

Love Came Down to a Little Manger

With Christmas just around the corner, we will probably receive and give many gifts.

While being in Romania, we have noticed that when people think about Christmas, they think about the birth of our Lord Jesus Christ, not about the gifts, parties, Santa Claus, or other common things. But the real reason for Christmas is acknowledged by nearly all Romanians.

Now, people say "Xmas" and give the excuse of just making an abbreviation, but really what they want to do is forget the true meaning of *Christ*mas! Christmas begins with Christ.

Romanian Christmas isn't just considered as a day off work or a day to go shopping, but they treat it like what it should be treated like—the season we remember our Savior's birth!

As we celebrate this Christmas season, may we *always* remember why we're celebrating it.

The Son of God loved us enough to willingly leave His throne in heaven, to come down to earth, and to be born in a manger, for a very special purpose. And the only reason He did it all was because He loves us. Merry *Christ*mas!

A Thankful Heart

God loves it when His children have a thankful heart toward Him.

Science proves that gratitude helps people feel more positive emotions, improves their health, helps them deal with adversity, and builds strong relationships.

Also, by studying the lives of thankful people mentioned in the Bible, most especially the life of Paul, we see that a thankful heart is the greatest motivator to staying strong and living for Christ.

The greatest characteristic anyone can obtain is a thankful heart.

When the glass is half empty to a negative person, the person with a thankful heart sees it half full. The entire perspective of a grateful person is different, and it is the best way to walk through life.

God wants us to be thankful to Him, in all situations, and the only way to remain thankful even in the hard times is to have a thankful heart and to remember that our joy does not depend on our circumstances but our joy is in the Lord and His fountain of joy never runs dry.

When the seas of life are crashing all around us, we need to remember that as Christians, we have the Holy Spirit of God living inside of us. He owns the seas and everything else. God's creation worships Him, and when He speaks peace, there is peace. We can always be thankful that He is our Master, Savior, and Friend. He is the Creator of the universe, and He is able to do anything.

So many times, we forget how much He has truly blessed us. All of us are unworthy of His grace and mercy, yet He blesses us time and time again! We need to keep in mind that if He never blesses us again, He is still so good.

How much do we thank Jesus for what He's done for us? Do we even thank Him for our salvation; for delivering us from hell, the torment and suffering that we deserve; and for giving us eternal life that no one can take away from us? Or do we take it for granted and treat it like it cost Him nothing? A thankful heart does not come by accident. It requires effort to kindle. But it is what God wants, and it is what we should want too.

If you feel like you haven't been blessed by God in a long while and you find it hard to be thankful, ask yourself this question, When was the last time that you simply spent time in prayer, thanking Him for all that He has done in the past? If you are not satisfied with your answer, I urge you to take a moment and just thank Him. It's never too late to say "Thank You!" but it does mean a lot more if we thank Him closer to the time He blessed us.

We all need to take a moment to just praise our Savior, not asking for anything, just coming before Him with a thankful heart. I can imagine the smile on God's face, when He's finally hearing the words that He's longed to hear for so long! "Thank You, Father. Thank You for saving me! Thank You for loving me. I do not deserve it! Thank You, Lord!" *This* is how you begin awakening the thankful heart that God wants you to have!

It is hard to find a genuinely grateful person. Many people are thankful when life is good and the skies are clear and sunny, but true thankfulness remains in the darkest nights and the strongest storms.

How to remain grounded steadfast in your thankfulness is simply this: remember Who is with you through the good and the bad and thank Him.

The Greatest Love of All

With Valentine's Day just around the corner, I am reminded day after day just how much we are all loved. It's amazing to know that the Creator of all things, the One Who has all things at His feet and controls it all, because of His love for us while we were yet sinners, came down to earth and took upon Himself the form of a servant and humbled Himself so much that He died on the cross for the sins of the world. He hung on the cross that I deserved and took my shame and punishment, all because of one thing—love.

The greatest example of love is the one that was demonstrated by Christ Jesus when He died for you and me!

The Lord has shown us what love truly is, and He wants us to demonstrate the same love to others.

The world today has many different definitions of love. But from the love displayed on Calvary, I see true love's characteristics of devotion, compassion, selflessness, humility, and patience.

Jesus gave His all for a world full of sinners, knowing that not all would receive Him, yet He still went through with it because He thought of those who would receive Him and be with Him for all eternity.

Love has many sacrifices and costs, but it is worth it all in the end!

A song I listen to called "I Love You from an Old Rugged Cross" says this:

> There was no hill too steep for me to climb,
> No road too long and hard to make you mine.
> I gave all I had to give,
> And it was worth the cost,
> To say I love you from an old rugged cross.

Think about where we would be today if Jesus had not paid the debt that we owed! I am so grateful that He died and rose again for my sins, and because of His great mercy I am loved, and I am the daughter of the King of kings! Oh, how amazing is His love for us! We can all receive instruction from this great example of love, and this Valentine's Day and every day, may we remember our first love—Jesus Christ!

Philippians 2:1–8; John 3:16; Matthew 22:37; Isaiah 53:3–7; Jeremiah 31:3; Ephesians 2:4; Ephesians 5:2; 1 John 4:10–11; 1 John 4:19; Romans 5:3–4; Romans 5:8

The Whole Armor of God

In Ephesians 6:11, we are told to put on the whole armor of God that we may be able to stand against the wiles of the devil. Then it goes on to say what that armor consists of in the following verses:

> Finally, my brethren, be strong in the Lord, and in the power of his might. Put on the whole armour of God, that ye may be able to stand against the wiles of the devil. For we wrestle not against flesh and blood, but against principalities, against powers, against the rulers of the darkness of this world, against spiritual wickedness in high places. Wherefore take unto you the whole armour of God, that ye may be able to withstand in the evil day, and having done all, to stand. Stand therefore, having your loins girt about with truth, and having on the breastplate of righteousness; And your feet shod with the preparation of the gospel of peace; Above all, taking the shield of faith, wherewith ye shall be able to quench all the fiery darts of the wicked. And take the helmet of salvation, and the sword of the Spirit, which is the word of God: Praying always with all prayer and supplication in the Spirit, and watching thereunto with all perseverance and supplication for all saints. (Ephesians 6:10–18)

Notice how it says we are to stand. In battle, if the enemy finds their adversary sitting or lying down in the grass, the enemy is most likely to obtain victory. But if we, soldiers of Jesus Christ (2 Timothy 2:3–4), are found standing and prepared for war, the enemy will sooner fall in defeat. Next, it gives us a description of what we need to be equipped with.

Our loins are to be girt about with truth. The Bible says many things about truth, but two things I think of when I see the word *truth* are is the Word of God (Psalm 119:160) and Jesus Christ (John 14:6).

Then it says we should have "the breastplate of righteousness." The Bible says that there is none righteous, no, not one. So how can we have on the breastplate of righteousness?

The only righteousness that we can put on is God's righteousness, and that is given to us the moment we put our faith in Jesus's finished work on Calvary (Romans 3:10, 22–24).

The passage goes on to say that our feet need to "be shod with the preparation of the gospel of peace" (1 Peter 3:15) (Colossians 4:6).

We should always be prepared to share the gospel with others. The Lord never forces someone to get saved. So if someone has heard the gospel yet still rejects it, that is on them. We are not held responsible for their response, but we are responsible to tell them the truth, and we should always be ready to share the truth with others.

It says the gospel of peace. This is describing the gospel, but why does it say "of peace"?

Until a person gets saved, they never truly have peace in their heart and mind. And they are not at peace with God until they accept the free gift of eternal salvation, which is only through Jesus Christ (Romans 5:1–2).

In the battle aspect, we should always be ready to settle for peace rather than more war. History is filled with unnecessary wars because people did not want to humble down and make peace, and because of this, more people lost their lives.

Then it says, "Above all, taking the shield of faith." *Above all* means that the things that are about to be mentioned are the most important pieces to this armor: "the shield of faith."

If we don't go into battle with the mindset of victory and we fight expecting to be defeated, then we are not fighting our hardest and best; therefore, we probably won't win! We need to have faith in our commanding officer and remember that we are more than conquerors through our Lord Jesus Christ, which giveth us the victory (1 Corinthians 15:57–58; Romans 8:37).

Next, it says to "take the helmet of salvation." A helmet protects our head. If something happens to our head, can we continue to fight? No. A helmet is vital for survival on this earth, while salvation is vital for where we spend eternity. Without salvation, our soul will spend eternity in hell. If you think that you can get to heaven without the helmet of salvation, you could not be farther from the truth. Eternity is far too long to be wrong, so we need to be sure that we have on the helmet of salvation.

It continues to tell us to take "the sword of the Spirit, which is the word of God."

When in battle, one cannot fight back without a weapon, and our weapon has already been provided to us. If we equip ourselves with it and know how to use it rightly, that weapon will be very defensive. But if we fail to bring it with us in combat, we are useless and can only run and hide from the enemy. Memorizing Scripture, applying it in context, and studying it is how we can equip ourselves with it.

Lastly, it says, "Praying always." This is so important! Throughout the Bible, we see many defeats when the people failed to pray and ask God for the wisdom they needed to win the victory. Perhaps this is the reason why of us are surrendering to the enemy and even in the smallest fights. When we fail to pray, we fail to put on the *whole* armor of God (James 4:1–3).

I hope that we are all encouraged to *daily* put on the *whole* armor of God, so that through our Lord, we can stand in victory!

Peace in the Midst of Burdens

At times, we feel burdened by the anxious cares that fill our hearts. Our minds spin with thoughts of fear and grief. God knows what we care about! God sees our hearts and knows exactly what we need. He has given us the joy sufficient to rejoice in the midst of our heavy hearts. We can cling to our hope in Him! It's in those times of struggles that we can run to Jesus for shelter, peace, and protection!

We can abide under the shadow of the Almighty God, Who is the Prince of peace, and the health of our countenance. He is our source of strength, even when we have nothing left. His supply of grace and peace, hope, joy, and strength will never run dry or even low!

Jesus is there to help us and uphold us when we're cast down in our souls. Psalm 42:5 says, "Why art thou cast down, O my soul? and why art thou disquieted in me? hope thou in God: for I shall yet praise him for the help of his countenance."

How often do we reach out to God for His comfort and peace through our stresses and cares that weigh us down? Because of our salvation through Jesus Christ, we have access to the throne of grace and can come unto Him when we are weary and heavy laden, knowing that His promise to give us rest will not fail. God wants to wrap His arms around us and remind us that we are safe in His embrace.

The first time I was told that God tells us 365 times not to fear, I was worried about something that hadn't even happened yet. Sometimes we worry about something that most likely won't even happen, but we worry ourselves with indefinite thoughts anyway. I am so glad that through it all, I can fix my eyes on the One Who holds tomorrow and knows what will happen both in my heart and in reality. God sees, knows, and controls everything down to the tiniest detail. We can trust Him to work everything together for good, just as He promised in His infallible Word!

Romans 5:1 reminds us that because we are justified by faith, we have peace with God through our Lord Jesus Christ. I am so grateful that not only do we have peace with God but we have peace through God! He gives us peace that passeth all understanding and grace that is sufficient even in our weakest moments! For this, we have every reason to rejoice!

Though the mountains are high and the waters are deep, God's love for us is so much greater, and His faithfulness will bring us through the hardships we face. The Lord upholds us with His right hand and will not leave us comfortless. He has come to us, and He will never leave us nor forsake us. The hand of God is not only holding us up but also holding on to us.

I find great comfort in Nehemiah's words, "The joy of the Lord is your strength." And I am reminded that I can rejoice because God's strength and joy is enough to keep me going even when the work is hard. No matter how heavy your burdens are, there is an open invitation to lay them at the feet of Jesus and leave them in His loving care. The peace that passeth all understanding can be yours when you cast all your cares upon Him, knowing that He cares for you!

If we have nothing else to rejoice in today, we have Jesus, and that will always be reason enough to rejoice!

Here is the chorus of a song I listen to that is a great reminder that the faithful Lover of our soul will never leave us to walk alone, not even for a moment:

> Never once did we ever walk alone!
> Never once did you leave us on our own!
> You are faithful! God, you are faithful!
> You are faithful! God, you are faithful!

Isaiah 41:10 and 13; Philippians 4:4–9; Psalm 55:22; Isaiah 9:6; John 14:27; Isaiah 61:10

Today

oday is the day of salvation (2 Corinthians 6:2).

Today is the day to be grateful (1 Thessalonians 5:18).

Today is the day to be a light (2 Corinthians 4:4).

Today is the day to bring glory to God (1 Corinthians 10:31).

Because we are not guaranteed tomorrow, we should live today to the fullest of God's purpose for the glory of God!

The Bible says that now it is high time to awake out of sleep (Romans 13:11). Now. Today.

Everything can change in one moment. In a moment. In the twinkling of an eye. Everything can change—that is, everything except our God, because He will never change! This should motivate us to do something for Him today!

All around us, there are lost souls in despair, with failing health and hurting hearts.

Inside their hearts, people are wondering if there is hope in this coronavirus epidemic, and the answer is yes! There is hope in the living God, the One Who on the cross shed His innocent blood, paying the debt that He did not owe, and arose from the dead three days later and is alive now and forevermore! We have a living hope because we have a living God!

For some states, the restrictions of the quarantine are coming to a close, and this is great!

Now, we have had our time to rest, and we are refreshed. This means that we should be excited to get back into the ministry of passing out tracts and meeting with people to be an encouragement. This virus has stirred up some people's hearts about eternity, and for some people, all they need now is a nudge—an invite to church, a gospel tract, someone to just tell them that Jesus loves them. You could be the one that nudges them! You could be the person who invites them to church or gives them a tract or maybe even prays with them. Just think, if you would simply take one step in their direction and reach out to them, their life could be changed forever. Jesus already did the hard part when He died for the sins of the world. We have the easy part. Don't allow the devil to stop you from reaching out, because you're afraid of how they'll respond. Remember, when someone rejects a gospel tract, a Bible, or an invitation to church, they're not rejecting you, but they're rejecting God.

We are called to be a light and to bring God glory and thanksgiving and to give Him our best. May we be exactly that today!

All Creation Sings

Satan likes for us to think that we are of little value to God, so we should value ourselves as worthless. This is not true, and the Bible clearly tells us that we are precious in the sight of God.

If we were as good as junk to God, He would not have died for us to give us an opportunity to be with Him in heaven forever, giving us a great escape from eternity in hell.

We can also see how much the Lord loves us through His creation.

Genesis 1 is a picture that is painted full of love. God spoke everything into existence, and it came forth at His command. When it came to man, He didn't just say, "Let there be man," and there was man. But we see in Genesis 1:27 that God stooped down to the ground and carefully molded man out of the dust, in the very image of God Himself! Wow! What a blessing that He would love us that much, knowing what was going to happen just two chapters later. Man would disobey his Creator.

Because of God's love for us, He gave us a free choice and offers a free gift of eternal salvation if we would only receive it. Romans 8:38–39 tells us how inseparable the love of Christ is to His children! No matter where we are or what we're going through in life, the love of Christ is there with us.

I had the opportunity of studying chemistry in school, and it has taught me many details of creation that I never thought of before. God not only put so many details into you and me, but the world around us is full of precision and design. Just a single atom is designed so meticulously that it took man until the eighteenth century to propose the idea of an atom. God is so omniscient that He knew exactly how things should be created in order to have the proper function for which He created them! Revelation 4:11 reminds us that everything that exists was created for the glory and pleasure of God.

Psalm 139:17–18 tells us that God has great thoughts about us, and it's so many that they are innumerable! You are of precious value to the Lord. He has great plans for your life, and despite what the world tells you, you are not an accident. But you were wonderfully designed by the God of all flesh (Psalm 139:14)!

> Order never comes from chaos unless some-
> one puts it together. (Mark Lowry)

This statement is so true and so simple to understand. It takes more faith to believe that everything happened by accident than to believe that an all-knowing and all-powerful God created it. God gave us His Word and preserved it through generations so that we can cling to it, believing in faith that it is true. Evolution gave us manmade, assumed theories that are based on a lie they created themselves to deny the truth that God's creation proclaims throughout His universe!

The birds sing praises to their Creator, the waves dance rejoicing of their Creator, the flowers bloom in the beauty of their Creator, and the leaves change their colors to glorify their Creator!

So should you and I praise our Creator! Just as the rest of creation is alive unto God and glorifies Him, we also should be alive unto God and glorify Him (Romans 6:11).

God values you greatly, He loves you with an everlasting love, and He wants you to praise Him.

Isaiah 40:26; Isaiah 45:5–8; Jeremiah 29:11; Jeremiah 31:3; Mark 10:16; Colossians 1:16; Romans 9:20–21; Psalm 107:8

In His All-Sufficiency

Too many days of my life I've spent trying to figure out and plan far into my future, but I always find that my plans change in some way or another. God wants to give us only the best, and it's not His will that we settle for less than His plan for our lives.

Being only in my late teenage years, I have already seen the Lord provide my biggest needs, time and time again! Because He is so gracious and so good, He's also provided so many of my wants and desires! Let this encourage you today that we have an all-sufficient Father Who is capable of all things and loves to bless His children and be praised from our grateful hearts.

Not only have I been provided for every time there are the smallest and biggest needs but many of my friends and family have as well. We all have the same God, so we can all be thankful for our Lord's goodness to us. Remember we don't deserve any of these blessings!

The same God Who gave me a camera last Christmas that I expected would take years to afford is the same God Who provides a paycheck every month. The God Who gave rest to a weary friend with cancer is the same God Who is now with her in glory! The same Father Who provided a friend's college tuition in one day's time is the same Father Who helps us when we stumble. The same Creator Who spoke the tallest mountain and the deepest ocean into existence is the same Creator Who made you and me! The same God Who provides airline tickets for missionaries to go home to their family on a consistent time frame is the same God Who will be with us not only on the mountaintops but also in the valleys. The same God Who delivered us from sin's penalty still delivers His salvation to those who receive Him.

If God parted the Red Sea for the children of Israel, calmed the storm on the Sea of Galilee, healed the incurable, and could feed over five thousand people, surely He is beyond capable to provide all your needs!

Matthew 6:25, 28–31 tells us that we should not worry about material things because God provides even for the lilies and the sparrows. Surely He will provide our needs if we trust Him to.

When we see a problem arise or a debt that we cannot possibly pay, we must remember to call upon the One Who is not limited to our humanly possible outcomes, but He is able to do exceedingly abundantly above all that we ask or think.

God saw the need for an eternal sacrifice to be made for our sins, so Jesus came down from heaven to die in our place, providing unending grace and eternal forgiveness. If He loves us that much, we have no reason whatsoever to doubt that He will provide in His all-sufficiency.

Psalm 116:1–2, 15; Genesis 22:8, 13; Exodus 14:13–31; Matthew 6:33; Philippians 4:6, 19; Romans 8:32; Luke 11:9–10

Purging My Thoughts

All my life I've struggled with negative thoughts about myself. I've questioned if God is really using me and my failures and if what I do is really good enough to please Him. One morning, while reading Psalm 35, the Holy Spirit showed me that I have been welcoming Satan into my thoughts by accepting his lies as the truth! Satan has been taking all my positive thoughts and turning them into judgmental and negative thoughts. Every day I have been persecuted by his sharp arrows of destruction, and every good thought God put into my heart, Satan has attacked and turned upside down into a giant of discontentment!

The only time God is disappointed in us is when we don't listen and follow His will! Even then, He is always trying to pull us back to the right path, by speaking to us through His spirit! God will never tear us down in discouragement, but rather He is pleased to see us serving Him with our all, and He is there to lift us up when we fall. God corrects, but God is gracious and loving.

God gave me a whole new light on this passage of Scripture, and it has opened my eyes to what has been going on for a very, very long time. Today, the purging begins! When a negative thought appears, I will ask God to open my eyes to see the truth about that thought, whether it is from Him, the spirit of truth, or if it is from the devil who is trying to blind the eyes of this world from the truth.

Before today, I've always looked over the parts of the Bible (especially Psalms) that talk about His enemies and foes, forgetting that I, too, have an enemy who is very real and needs to be seen for who he is! He is an adversary not only to me but to all of us! He loves to deceive and destroy and is not worthy of our attention. Satan hates truth, which is why he loves to disguise himself!

Don't fall into the nets he has laid for you, don't be oblivious to who he is, and don't give him any part of your life! If he can get in the smallest crack of your heart, he will. And he will slowly eat away at your positivity, your joy, your knowledge of truth, your relationships, and your walk with God! Fight for your heart's purity! Ask God to purge you! Guard your thoughts because they start in your heart!

Read this passage, recognizing what your enemy is doing to you, and pray that God will help you fight for your heart's purity and truth.

Psalm 35

Panoramic Faith

When we imagine our life as a panorama and we are currently in the center, we can look to the left to view our past and see how God worked things out for His good and made a way for us to overcome every obstacle in our path. Now, we look ahead at where we are now and see how we just have to stand still and watch God work in us and through us. Then, we can boldly have faith in the fact that we can trust Him to paint the rest of our life with fullness and beauty.

Hebrews 11:1 says that faith is what we cannot see. Faith is having confidence that God will work everything out in the future, for His glory and honor, and He will perform beautiful miracles in our future just like He has in our past and even presently today.

Realize a panorama photograph is only ruined by a change in position or motion or a glitch in the camera. We have nothing to fear because the Bible says that Jesus is the same yesterday, today, and forever. His position will never change, and He will never have a glitch or fall asleep on the job. The Bible says that He faints not, nor is He weary. We have every reason to trust God with our future. Our past is reason enough to have faith in God for the rest of our life to be provided for and taken care of and that He will be right there with us until death and even after death we will be with Him in eternity.

May we trust God for our future and die daily to our worldly worries and cares, because we have seen His provision time and time again.

Hebrews 13:8; Jeremiah 29:11; Psalm 37:25; Matthew 6:25–34; Hebrews 11:1; Hebrews 4:16

Perspective

In a world filled with things, we often lose sight of the people around us. We get so focused on material things, our possessions, our needs, and our comforts that we lose sight of the fact that we are to be concerned about people! Christ came into the world to save people, not things! Everything that we have, hold, and hope to earn on this earth will all vanish away and be forgotten. People leave lasting memories and impacts on our lives, and all people have an eternal soul. We walk through the grocery store with only food and products on our minds, while people pass all around us—people who need to see someone with a smile on their face and who need to know that there's so much more to life than eating, drinking, sleeping, and dying.

Jesus walked the earth for around thirty-three years, and His life has impacted all mankind. He made a difference. He did so much more than we can ever do, but we should all do more than we are doing now! If you knew that the year of 2022 would be your last year to live, what would you cut out of your life, and what would you start doing? I highly doubt it would be to work more or buy more things. It would be to spend more time with people, and I hope to tell more people about Jesus!

Anymore, we see someone looking thin and sickly, we cringe at the dirt on their clothes, and walk as far away from them as we can just so we don't feel uncomfortable. We have no idea what they're going through! Who are we to judge other people? Who made us the evaluator of persons? The only person we are to judge is ourselves, yet we find so little time to do that!

No matter what assumptions we make about other people, we can't fix them. We can only fix our own problems, but first we must acknowledge them and humbly bring them to the Lord.

If we would just look at people through the eyes of grace, the eyes of compassion, and a tender heart, then we would grow our love and burden for people!

We all have problems that we need to work on, but only we can change our attitude and our actions, not others.

When we decide to see people through God's perspective—the eyes of grace, compassion, and patience—we choose to show them the love of Christ. We look beyond their outward appearance and share the glorious gospel with them.

The Bible says "whosoever," so we ought to tell them that includes them! It included us, did it not? So why do we get saved, praise the Lord, and hide our light under a bushel?

I truly believe that every country needs missionaries, including America. The rates of suicide, murder, drug abuse, and alcoholism are sky-high all across our own country! And what are we doing about it? We're just hiding out in our little comfort zone, thinking of ourselves more highly than we ought to think, while so many people outside our doorstep are hurting, hungry, cold, confused, addicted to sin, and dying without a hope! I ask again, What are we doing about it!?

I encourage you to go listen to the song "Through the Eyes of Christ" by Ron Hamilton.

Broken Vessels

*T*oday you may feel like a broken piece of pottery, a beautiful flower vase that's been crushed into a thousand shattered pieces. People have even told you that you're not worth anything to God now that you're broken or that you're not pretty enough to be loved by Him, the God of all the beauties of creation. In your doubts and broken heart, let me be the one to tell you that God still uses broken vessels.

We often read through the Bible about the people who did great things for God, and in our minds we see them as perfect people without problems or scars. Although this is just our human nature to imagine things in the way they truly aren't, the truth is still the truth—that no one is perfect.

No one is without scars, and no one is without problems. Whether you're a Christian or not, we have all sinned. And because we live in a sinful world, we have heartache, pain, and tears. And every one of us has scars. But when we yield ourselves to the Master, the Potter Who created us in the womb and knew us even before then, He fixes us and puts our broken pieces back together. God wants to use us, His creation and His handiwork, for His glory. He invests so much into us He deserves our life, our everything, no matter how broken we may be.

God is a God of new beginnings, and He loves to take our shame and turn it into a beautiful masterpiece to bring Him glory!

Coming to Christ is so simple. The only hard part is humbling ourselves enough to come.

This statement is so true, "God wants you to come just as you are, but He does not want you to leave just as you came." You cannot be touched by God and not experience some kind of change. He has only love in His heart for you and longs to do good things in your life if you'll let Him. Yes, it's hard to put all your broken shards out in the open light, where you can see all the pain and the shame that you felt to get them. But when God takes those pieces and starts to work with each piece, He puts one piece with the other and keeps adding to it until it's back together again, and it's even more beautiful as it's ornate beauty shines from its freshly polished edges. God can take something so broken and crushed and make it into a masterpiece, but He must have all the pieces. Are all the pieces of your shattered heart surrendered to God, the One Who can fix you and bless you with joy and love that will never die or walk away? The God Who loves you so much that His Son died so that you could live and is alive today and loves you despite how broken and unwanted you feel? He longs that you come to Him, for rest and joy and blessings. He wants to be your completer.

Psalm 34:18; Psalm 51:17; John 14:8; John 14:27

Comfort Zone

This is my comfort in my affliction:
for thy word hath quickened me.

—Psalm 119:50

Our comfort is something we all seek after, is it not? Here, David said where he found his comfort, and we can all find comfort in it as well—the Word of God.

If we are in affliction, like David was, all we have to do is get in the Word of God, and we will be comforted. Satan wants to afflict us with fear and many waters around us, but God is the God of all comfort, and Jesus is called the Prince of peace. He has sent us the Holy Spirit to comfort us and to teach us. So since we naturally like to be in our comfort zone, why is it so hard to read the Bible? The answer is this—God's Word is truth, and the devil hates truth and will do all he can to keep you and me out of the Word of truth! The devil wants to cripple you and paralyze you, and just like a spider captures its food, Satan wants to entangle you in the sticky, miserable sin that he weaves to look attractive. Don't be mesmerized by the outside appearance of Satan's nets and traps for you!

Instead, walk with the God of all comfort and the Giver of life, and remember to thank Him for the great comfort we have in Him and in His Word!

All God's Word is comforting because the same God Who was in control in Genesis 1:1 is still on the throne today and He will forever be the Most High God. Let God comfort you through His Word, and His Holy Spirit will multiply that comfort, and remember that you were bought and saved by the Prince of peace.

Psalm 119:2; Psalm 119:11; Psalm 119:24; Psalm 119:50; Psalm 119:62; Psalm 119:105; Psalm 119:160; Psalm 119:162; Psalm 119:165

Look Up!

When you feel as if the devil is impeding your every move, look to Jesus, Who holds all the power and has already overthrown the devil! In Christ, you, too, can have the victory over the devil's nets and snares, if you'll just look up to your Deliverer!

When Satan pours rain on your parade, keep singing through the thunderstorm. And when he discourages you from doing what's right, when he distracts you with temporal treasures and echoes your mind with bad news, calling you to a life of misery, look to God. With his daily oppression, you are tired and angry, but instead, God wants us to be a light and a beacon of hope. Satan knows his time is short and wastes no time seeing that he will soon be cast down, but he works extra hard to win as many people as he can to himself and away from God and away from the truth.

When Satan calls on you to give up and to fall into his trap, pick up your sword and fight him off. He may not retreat right away, but he will not steal your joy. And once he sees you're a fighter, he will eventually leave you alone and go fight someone else in that moment.

When we use the weapons God has given us, we not only beat the devil, but we grow in the Lord. And this pleases our Savior in Whom we can overcome the devil's intent to destroy our life, our joy, our purity, and our testimony.

So on the days when you find yourself on the battle's front, use every weapon God's given you and fight for your life, for your home, and for the ones who look up to you and put a smile on God's face by using the weapons He's given you.

The spirit of God lives inside of you, and He will help you know how to use your weapons and be your guide and comfort in the battle. Fight, look up, and overcome!

James 4:7; Hebrews 4:12; Psalm 112:7; Psalm 119:11; Proverbs 29:25; Ephesians 4:27; Philippians 4:13; Colossians 1:11; 1 Timothy 6:12; 2 Timothy 3–4

Hope through a COVID-Stricken World

This morning, as I was putting the dishes away, I was listening to the news and was getting very disgusted at the way people are handling the whole lockdown situation, Thanksgiving being only those in your household, the unproven vaccine coming, and the election mess. I find myself asking God for grace every time I open my mouth. It is so easy to be negative all the time, although I know as a Christian I have so much to be positive about! After hearing of the bad news all around us, I started reading my Bible, looking for a positive thought. And the verse that stood out to me was in Romans 12:12, which says, "Rejoicing in hope; patient in tribulation; continuing instant in prayer."

In these perilous days, we must not be discouraged by our current circumstances, but we must remember our future and rejoice in our hope.

Our future is in the hands of God Almighty, Who is not slack concerning His promises.

Our future, as promised, is in heaven, where we'll be with Jesus forever. There will be no more viruses, and bad news is never reported. We'll never sorrow or die, but we'll be with Jesus for all eternity. This is our future, and we have a hope that is strong in this storm.

What do we pray for? Do we pray that God will deliver us out of trouble? Do we ask God why? Do we waste our time in prayer, complaining? Or do we give Him glory and honor and praise, with a thankful heart? God has given us so much to be thankful for, and yet we let our circumstances disrupt our praise. Let me encourage you to read 1 Thessalonians 4:13–18 every time you start to complain about the angry waves around us, as this will turn your perspective and you will begin to shout out to God in thanksgiving that what He has promised, He will do!

Just beyond those encouraging verses is a charge—a charge to be the light that this world so desperately needs. In 1 Thessalonians 5:4–6 we are reminded who we are in Christ. We are the children of light, and we are in a dark and perverse world, whose only hope and only light is God our Father! We have the Light living inside of us, so why do we stand around moping and complaining like others who have to hope? Christians ought to be the happiest people on earth, because our happiness does not come from our circumstances, but our joy is in the Lord Who made heaven and earth!

We have the light! What are we doing with it? Are we passing it along, or are we hiding it under a bushel and keeping it to ourselves?

The Bible also says in Hebrews 2:3, "How shall we escape, if we neglect so great salvation." This verse speaks for itself. This world is full of wickedness, strife, and fear. And it will only get worse. Without accepting Jesus Christ as your Savior, your future is in hell where there is only evil, fear, torment, and wrath forever. There is no escape after death, but you can accept that so great salvation if you humble yourself before God and accept Him. He is the only way out of your past, present, and future! All you have to do is accept Him.

For those of us who have accepted this free gift of salvation, we are in Christ, and our hope is in Him. We should be shining the light God has given us and remember that even though we can find grace at the throne of God, we shouldn't leave as we came (complaining) but we should leave praising God and sharing the good news that we have in Him!

Philippians 2:15; 2 Timothy 1:7; 1 Thessalonians 5:16–18; Colossians 4:5–6; Colossians 3:12–15; Ephesians 4:29; Ephesians 5:16; Hebrews 4:16

A Humble Servant

One cannot be in the ministry and have results if they do not have a humble heart. A leader cannot be a true leader without first being a servant.

A servant is someone who does things for others before helping himself, one who takes himself from the highest rank of importance and puts himself at the bottom, so that he can best serve the needs of others. A humble servant recognizes that he is unworthy and that apart from Christ he is nothing.

Paul called himself a servant of Christ, and he was a great servant of Christ for many reasons, but I believe it was mainly because of his humility. Everything he did and said, he made sure it was known that it was only by the grace of God that he was doing it. Paul was not afraid to get on his knees in prayer or to sing praises to God aloud or to be physically hurt so that others could hear what God wanted them to know. Paul knew that it wasn't in what he could do but in what God could do through him!

So many movies focus on the people who are the opposite of how most people really truly are. They try to deceive us to think that we are good people who need to think of ourselves first for a change. They tell us that we would do anything to help someone else out and that we are people who never say no to humbly helping another. Sadly, I don't believe this is the kind of people we are.

From what I can see in myself a lot of the time and in the world around me is a "me attitude" and inexcusable selfishness and pride. The Bible says that God hates pride, so we ought to search our hearts and ask God to cleanse us and make us genuinely humble and effective servants for Him and His glory! So many of us want to make ourselves look good to others, to ourselves, and to God. But God sees right through the facade.

Oftentimes, we see others living in sin, and we tend to judge them and congratulate ourselves that we are not like them. We need to let the judging and lifting up, up to God!

Did you ever notice how the Bible says to examine ourselves? So why do we twist that to say we should examine others?

Our flesh is naturally proud and selfish, but we need to listen to the spirit of God inside of us and be humble before God and before others. We must never think of ourselves more highly than we think of others! This is when pride sets in and begins to rule our hearts, then our actions, and ultimately our testimony.

We are all sinners saved by the grace of God! Before we got saved, we were no better than the drunk living on the street or the rich man who gave none to the poor. We must not forget where we were before Jesus saved us, and we need to give all the glory and praise to God for His grace by which we are saved!

May we all take a step back and notice the needs of others and do something about it, serving one another and serving Christ in humility and in love.

Galatians 1:24; Acts 20:19; Ephesians 3:8; 1 Corinthians 15:9–10; 1 Timothy 1:15; James 4:6; James 4:10; Proverbs 15:33; Proverbs 29:23; Philippians 2:3–11; Luke 14:11

The Purpose of Personal Devotions

Lord, help us to take time out of our day for You, because You are the One Who gives us all our days.
We remember

- the blessing it is to others, (It is an encouragement to other Christians, to see you living your life in communication with God and seeking out His will for your life.)
- the joy it brings to God, and (Just like when you hear from your best friend who hasn't spoken to you in a while, it thrills the Lord's heart when we take time to talk to Him! After all that He does for us, our appreciation to Him is the best thing we can give back.)
- the satisfaction it gives to us. (We are all thirsty, thirsty for more blessings or more knowledge, for a clearer picture of God's will for our life, or for the sun to shine again in our stormy life. God's Word is the most refreshing and revealing thing we can feel inside of our hearts and in our hands as a tangible item. It is the very way the Holy Spirit proves things to us, that what He is convicting you of in your heart is really there and needs to be noticed.)

If we expect our spiritual life to grow and flourish, we must water it and give it sunshine, and we must never take for granted our time spent with God.

When you spend time alone with God, it is like spending time alone with your best friend, giving you that one-on-one time that strengthens your relationship and deepens your love for them.

The Lord wants to hear from you. He is waiting for you to call out to Him and for you to come sit and talk with Him. He has the water and sunshine ready to give you.

If a plant only gets five minutes of sunshine a day and a few drops of water, the plant will not give much fruit. The same is true with our spiritual life. We can't spend five minutes in the Bible and expect an apple by the end of the day; it needs time, labor, and nurturing.

In this ever-so-busy and crazy world we live in, it is essential that we come away and spend some quiet time with God, recollecting why we are in this race and Whom our eyes should be fixed upon.

Mark 6:31–32 tells us that Jesus sees the need for rest. God Himself rested on many occasions, and the first time we see it mentioned was on the seventh day of creation. Don't you think that if God rested and if Jesus told His disciples to rest, we ought to rest as well?

Psalm 46:10 says, "Be still, and know that I am God: I will be exalted among the heathen, I will be exalted in the earth." The word *still* here means "to stop, to make quiet, to calm."

When everything around you is moving so fast and the voices in your head remind you of your past failures or of the present fears you should run from, when all you feel like doing is quitting, be still. Come and rest awhile, and spend some time alone with your Redeemer. You will walk away refreshed with a new song and be refocused on Him.

Psalm 40:2–3; Psalm 23; Psalm 93:4; Exodus 20:11; 2 Corinthians 1:3–4; Isaiah 41:10; Psalm 138:3; John 16:33; Philippians 4:6–7

We Forgot

We have become like Israel! We have forgotten God and have turned to fulfill our own desires!

Even the priests and prophets who were supposed to be the spiritual leaders transgressed against God, and it says they didn't even know God!

God brought us to our free land and stood with us through the wars and battles we faced, but even after all that, we have forgotten God and have made other things into our gods!

We, too, have forgotten God. And when a problem comes on the scene, we ask God to deliver us, but why should He? We have changed our glory for that which doth not profit, and we expect God to act as though we are innocent?

When we stand before God, we *will* be ashamed, if we do not get it right now!

Don't waste another minute of the life God has given you bringing shame and displeasure to Christ, and start giving Him all the glory He deserves!

Verse 37 clearly states that the things we are confident in, if they are not the Lord's, they will be rejected and will not profit us at all and we cannot expect to profit in them!

Only God blesses! Our confidence needs to be in only God!

God has been blessing me with so many things over the past year, for my first home! For this, I am extremely grateful, but there was a time when I was so focused on gathering things for this big event that I allowed my focus to shift toward these things, rather than the Giver of them!

In that moment, I remember falling on my knees, asking God to forgive me and help me keep my focus on Him. Without Him and His help, I would have nothing, I would be nothing, and I would not be strong enough to take these steps of faith! Every day, I wonder how I will live alone, how I will sleep at night without frightful thoughts keeping me awake. But that's when I'm reminded that I am not alone! I have the Word of God to cling to and rehearse through my mind on those sleepless nights. "I will never leave thee nor forsake thee…" "I will not leave you comfortless…" "The LORD is my strength and my shield…" "The LORD is my shepherd…" "The LORD is on my side; I will not fear: what can man do unto me?"

God has proved Himself faithful, so why should I forget Him now?

But it is so easy to get distracted by material things. Faith is the substance of things hoped for, the evidence of things not seen. We can't touch heaven yet. We can't even see all the beauty it holds yet, but our flesh wants things now. It doesn't like to wait for something we can't enjoy fully now. Our flesh wants to live in the here and now. But we are to set our minds on things above and to lay up for ourselves treasures in heaven, not down here on earth where they will vanish and burn away.

The reason we don't give to missions like we should is because we are so focused on our own comfort and getting material things that we forget we are to share the gospel with others! If God didn't ask you to go to a foreign country and preach the gospel, then the least you can do is support others who do! If God lays it on your heart to give toward the spreading of God's Word and the very gospel that saved you from hell, then by all means, give what the Lord tells you to give, and let the rest up to God!

It is amazing how much God can bless you if you'll just do what He tells you to do!

When we tell God we can't do something, He might just take you out of your comfort zone to prove to you that He can!

Ecclesiastes 11:1; Jeremiah 2; Jeremiah 9:23–24

Fear: The Fiery Darts of the Wicked

Many of us do not fully understand the impact that fear has on our lives. Fear brings anxiety, and anxiety creates stress, and stress brings health problems, which can lead to death. So why fear death, when fear itself can bring death? We need to remember that God hath not given us the spirit of fear but of power and of love and of a sound mind (2 Timothy 1:7).

God is the God of peace and of life, not of fear and death!

If God intended for our lives to be filled with fear, He wouldn't have given us hope and peace in Him.

Situations around us are pressing fear into our hearts, and some of us don't even realize it!

Do we fear what may happen tomorrow? Do we fear what America will look like in a year? Are we fearful about getting sick with any type of virus? Are we afraid of dying? Are we living in subjection to fear?

Fear—a powerful thing the devil uses as his deadly weapon. The devil uses it to control us and to destroy us! If we aren't mindful to use our weapons, we will be tormented by his weapon of fear! God has instructed us how we are to fight. We are to fight valiantly with the whole armor of God.

The shield of faith is what quenches all the fiery darts of the wicked! So where is our faith? Mark 4:40 says it best, "And he said unto them, Why are ye so fearful? how is it that ye have no faith?"

Once we begin to fear, we are caught in the snare of torment because the Bible says that fear hath torment.

1 John 4:17–18 tells us this, "Herein is our love made perfect, that we may have boldness in the day of judgment: because as he is, so are we in this world. There is no fear in love; but perfect love

casteth out fear: because fear hath torment. He that feareth is not made perfect in love."

How are we to fight the devil's darts of fear in our daily lives? It tells us right here that we need perfect love to cast out fear, and that love is made perfect how? "That we may have boldness," boldness, confidence, hope, faith. Each one of those words is connected and means almost the same thing. If we want to have perfect love in order to cast out fear, we must have faith in the One Who is love and Who is perfect—faith that He is in control, faith that He is more powerful than the uncertainties of life, faith that He has delivered us from eternal death, faith that He is coming back to take His bride home with Him, and faith that He will never leave us nor forsake us! We need to have boldness in the day of battle and give thanks to God, which giveth us the *victory*!

Don't let the devil use fear to destroy the victorious life you can live in Jesus Christ!

Proverbs 3:25–26; Romans 8:15; Hebrews 13:6; Proverbs 29:25; Psalm 91:4–6; John 14:27; Psalm 27:1, 3

Our Gracious God

*H*ow often do we praise God for Who He is?

Truly, we have every reason to praise Him for what He's done for us, but what about for Who He is? Do we thank Him for His power, His knowledge, and His sovereignty?

God is so great, and David (who was noted as a man after God's own heart) said this:

> Thine, O Lord is the greatness, and the power, and the glory, and the victory, and the majesty: for all that is in the heaven and in the earth is thine; thine is the kingdom, O Lord, and thou art exalted as head above all. Both riches and honour come of thee, and thou reignest over all; and in thine hand is power and might; and in thine hand it is to make great, and to give strength unto all. Now therefore, our God, we thank thee, and praise thy glorious name. (1 Chronicles 29:11–13)

David gave God the praise and glory He deserves. David not only praised God when He was alone, but David said this in the midst of a congregation. David made sure that others knew Who God is and how great God is. David didn't boast about himself to others, but David boasted of God. God was the One Who made David to be king, God was David's ever-present help in trouble, and David was determined to exalt God for all that He had done and for all that God was to him!

What is God to you? Do you find your safe refuge in Him? Does God hear your cries? Did God save you from your sins? Do you have a Father Who delights in blessing His children? Is God your only source of strength? Do you remember where God brought you from and what He's brought you through? Does God give you the ability to work and the provision to pay your bills?

We all need to praise God for Who He is to us and for all the things He's done!

God has not failed me one time! He has always come through, and no matter what time He answers your prayer, are you watching and waiting for His answer? Are you fully trusting Him to hear and attend to your cries? God is an on-time God, Who answers every one of our prayers!

All that God does for us can be summed up into one word—grace.

Grace! We all know the song "Amazing Grace," but do we know the depth of what God's grace really is? It's so deep that I don't even fully understand it yet. But every day it seems to go deeper and deeper, covering my sins and burying them in the depths of the sea, as His waves of grace cover my soul and overflow into my everyday life.

Grace is defined as the unmerited favor of God toward us. We don't deserve one bit of this grace, yet we cannot escape it. The grace that was there at the cross when Jesus paid for my sins, the grace that was there the night I accepted Christ as my personal Savior, the grace that is with me every day, it's the same grace that we have access to every day.

Every time there's grace, there's also love and mercy. Think of it like an alloy (combination) of grace, love, and mercy. It is impossible to break these apart, and this alloy is strong because they are bonded together with the unbreakable bond of the blood of Jesus Christ. Grace, love, mercy—they're all here. And although we do not deserve grace, love, or mercy, we cannot escape them, and they keep multiplying every breath that we're given.

As we think about Who God is, may we praise Him and never forget how gracious He is.

We can always give God glory for not just His attributes but for His ever-present grace, love, and mercy.

Psalm 71:19–22; Psalm 113; Revelation 4:11; Genesis 6:8; Romans 5:20; 1 Corinthians 15:10; 2 Corinthians 12:9; Ephesians 1:7; Jeremiah 31:3; Psalm 36:5

The Significant Truth

I wanted to share another subject with you today, but the Lord dealt with my heart to conceal it. We hear so much about the recent deaths of people who suddenly took a turn for the worse.

Though many of us recognize the reason, there is an even greater problem that people need to hear. Where are those souls spending eternity right now? It ought to break our hearts for the people who died without Jesus! It ought to spread a desire among us to tell someone about Jesus today! We see people are dying suddenly, but are we sharing the true light with those who are still alive? They may not be open to reports about the cause of these deaths, but I believe God has a purpose for all this evil around us. Satan means it for evil, but God wants to use it for good.

Perhaps the fields are ripe and ready to harvest, but the laborers are few (as stated in Matthew 9:37). Are the laborers few because we are so stuck on another truth? Yes, the truth of the matter is important, but more important is the eternity of the souls around us!

If we come in contact with ten people a day and tell one person about Jesus every day, we are doing the very least that we can do to reach people with the gospel of Jesus Christ!

I encourage you to pick up a stack of gospel tracts from your church's supply and challenge yourself to hand out every single one of those before the end of the week.

More souls are perishing every day, but what are we doing about it? It seems we have lost our passion for souls when we laugh at the death of the wicked, but we seem to have forgotten that we were the one bound for hell! We were the one without the gospel of Jesus Christ! We were the one condemned to eternal punishment! Until someone reached out to us and showed us the saving grace of our Lord Jesus Christ! That same grace is what needs to be shared with the souls around us! "How then shall they call on him in whom they have not believed? and how shall they believe in him of whom they have not heard? and how shall they hear without a preacher?" (Romans 10:14).

Getting the gospel out is what we are called to do as Christians! We aren't called to preach against the deceit of man. That's the job of the Holy Spirit inside of each individual, after they're saved. But we are called to be servants of God, serving Him in love and fighting through the evil around us, keeping our focus on Him, and sharing the glorious gospel as a light shining all around us!

The answer to all the deception and lies that are being spread far more than the actual coronavirus, my friend, is Jesus Christ! If just one soul is saved from eternal hell today, let it be because you took the time to tell them about Jesus!

The harvest truly is plenteous, but the laborers are few. Don't just pray for God to send someone else to reach them. Be that servant, that laborer, that ambassador of Jesus Christ! Someone's soul depends upon it!

John 10:10; 2 Corinthians 5:17–21; Genesis 50:20; John 3:15–19; Matthew 5:14–16; John 14:1–6; John 8:32; John 16:33; Matthew 9:36–38; Philippians 2:14–16; 2 Corinthians 4:3–6; Romans 12:21; Romans 10:14–15; Ephesians 5:15–17; 1 Corinthians 9:14; Proverbs 18:19–21

We Are the Next Generation

Teens and young people, we need to wake up to the fact that we are the next generation! It's up to us to keep following God's plan and to run the race that our parents and grandparents have started! We must stand firm on the truth, not wavering, but we must declare that "As for me and my house, we will serve the Lord." We cannot back down when face-to-face with the enemy. We must fight the good fight of faith.

We can hold fast to the truth at all times! It is always true and will never fail, and it is the greatest weapon we have in this life! It is the truth that reminds us we have a hope and a future, the truth that shows us how to be saved, the truth that declares the glory and goodness of God, the truth that brings us closer to our Savior, the truth that tells us our life has great purpose, and the truth that encourages people to come to Jesus and live for Him!

The Bible is God's true preserved Word to mankind, and it has never been completely destroyed or forgotten! God's Word has always been blessed, and God blesses us when we read it! There are times when I am just too tired to read it, so I go about my day as normal, but if I only knew all the blessings I missed out on! When I forget to read my Bible in the morning, my day is filled with strife and anxiety! Reading God's Word gives peace and comfort and reminds me to show grace and compassion to others, just as Christ does to me every single day.

Reading the Bible puts my perspective in the right place, on Jesus. When I neglect to listen to what God has to say, my entire day feels like I accomplished nothing worthwhile. If only I had read my Bible for just ten minutes, I would've been one more day more in love with Jesus and one more day deeper into His Word.

A generation that will stand up and serve the Lord needs to communicate with the Lord and let Him communicate to us. If we don't know what our Master wants us to do, how will we know to do it? If we don't ask for wisdom and guidance, how will we expect to find our way through this dark world? If only more of us, the next generation, would stand up and say, "As for me and my house, we will serve the Lord."

This is not only directed to us teenagers but to all of us no matter what our age is!

Grandparents, lead your grandchildren closer to Jesus by the way you act and speak.

Parents, take time to personally pray for and with your kids. Let them know they're more important than the tasks in your day, and let them know through your actions that you're praying for them.

The Bible says, "If my people will humble themselves..." We are the people who are to humble themselves and lead people to Christ.

No matter how old you are, God wants you to share Him with others! Let's raise up the next generation to serve the Lord, and let's be the next generation that serves the Lord!

1 Timothy 4:12; 1 Timothy 6:12; Joshua 24:15; Psalm 62:6

Shew Forth His Praise

Read: Psalm 78:1–8.

First of all, notice it says "my people." So many of us are quick to say, "We the people of the United States of America," but who we are in Christ is more important than our earthly citizenship.

We the people saved by God's grace are told in the following verses that to raise up the next generation to follow Christ, we are to set an example for them and to show them all that God has done for us!

I have never been a fan of history, but one thing I do love hearing about is how God has worked in people's lives! That's the history we should all concern ourselves with! The history of what God has done for our parents and our grandparents and even further down the line. Even if your family didn't grow up in a Christian home, I'm sure there were still things God did to try to get their attention, and we can take notice of what God did and be encouraged that He is still working today!

Verse 4 says, "We will not hide them from our children," and then it goes on to say that we will shew forth His strength.

What has the Almighty God done for you? Can you think back to a time when your life was in ruins and there was no possible way known to man for you to escape? But God (amen!) stepped in and did the impossible and blessed you with a miracle and set your feet upon the solid rock!

For some, God gave them a child or a spouse. Maybe it was healing or a special caregiver or perhaps a promotion at work or a good-paying job. The list could go on and on, because with God, the possibilities are endless! He is the God of the impossible. Because He created the laws of physics, of course He can bend them to fit His plan! Nothing you've faced before was too big for God, and nothing you're up against today is too great for God to do the impossible!

Our young people need to know that there is a God Who still does miracles, and He deserves our praise! What do we need to tell the next generation? What has God done for us that we need to share with others?

Psalm 62:7; Psalm 150:6; Psalm 111:4; Psalm 45:17

Defeated?

o you feel defeated today? Truth is I do. Reality is Christianity doesn't exempt us from problems and discouragement, but it does give us a solid hope and constant friend through it all, and that is Jesus! Maybe you feel discouraged because you've lost a loved one or the words "We've done all that we can do" keep running through your mind.

Maybe you received some devastating news or just simply want all these restrictions to be lifted. Whatever cloud of discouragement hangs over your life today, let me just remind you that above that cloud is the God Who is greater than what you're facing. Nothing has taken Him off His throne of omnipotence, and nothing ever will! He will always hold the power that you need to get through this storm!

I refer to hard times as "storms" not only because I've heard many others use that term before but because storms have rain, just like our tears. Storms have darkness, just like our uncertainty. Storms have streaks of lightning, just like our aching broken hearts. Storms have thunder, just like the roaring voices inside our heads telling us "We're defeated." Storms—they're no fun to go through, and tears and sorrow are hardly ever welcomed with a smile. But I am comforted by the fact that my Lord, Who sees every tear that falls, hears every cry and knows the deepest hurtful strike that my heart has felt. He has calmed many storms. I remember when He spoke "Peace, be still" to the raging seas, controlling my fears at the sound of His voice. I also remember the times when He's let the storm go on but walked me through it hand in hand, telling my heart, "Peace, be still."

We wish we wouldn't have to walk through storms and face the tempest of the deep waters that cover our hearts with tears, but we can always stand strong and be encouraged that our omnipotent Savior never leaves our side.

While the thick clouds above us cast a shadow over us, do we ever think of the times the storms didn't come? The sunny days? Those times when life was okay? We seem to always lose sight of the sunshine moments while going through a dark downpour of distress. Another thing that comforts me is the simplest and shortest verse of the Bible, John 11:35, which says, "Jesus wept."

Two words that hold a powerful message. This took place after Lazarus had died and just before Jesus brought him back to life. Keep in mind Jesus knew what was about to happen, but He didn't scold Mary and Martha, but rather they scolded Jesus for not being there to heal Lazarus! Maybe this was just them telling Him that they believed that He could've saved Lazarus. I don't know. There are two different ways of looking at it, but Jesus didn't tell them to suck it up and stop crying. He cried with them. This is a great comfort to me because I am reminded that it's okay to cry, but I'm also reminded to rejoice because my God cares for me!

I can always rejoice because I have Jesus with me, and even though He has not lost the power to raise someone from the dead, I don't have to wait for the resurrection of the dead to rejoice. But I can rejoice because the Comforter has come and He himself is alive forevermore!

We need to remember that even if we feel defeated and chained to this cloud above us, we can cry out to God and ask Him to remind us of the sunny days and walk us through this storm.

John 11; John 14:16; Hebrews 13:5

Good News!

*D*o you ever wonder why all we ever hear about is the bad news? Some could say, "Because there's so much of it!" Others might say, "Because the media doesn't share the good news!" And some may even say, "Because there is no good news!"

Although some of these answers are true, I want you to know that in a world full of wickedness and overflowing with bad news, there is *good news*!

God has not stopped working because of the increasing evil! No, God is not intimidated by the things that we are discouraged by, nor does the devil make God tremble!

You're probably still asking, "Where is the good news?" It's right over there on a shelf, collecting dust! It's hidden inside the heart of the Christian who doesn't remember the last time he went to church! And it's right ready to be shared with the world, if only we would let it get out of our depressed and intimidated heart and let it shine and bring hope to a world who needs it now more than ever!

The devil is working overtime, but God hasn't stopped working in our hearts, and maybe He is calling you to work overtime and share the good news! We have the good news, and what are we doing with it?

How will others remember that there is good news if we don't let the revival start? There doesn't have to be a church revival for you to have a personal revival. If each of us would let God change us from the inside out, in time, we may see a church revival or even a national revival!

What does *revival* mean? Two definitions of *revival* are "An instance of something becoming popular, active, or important again" and "To bring back to life." Remember another instance where we were brought back to life? Paul reminds us in Ephesians 2:1–10 that we were dead in our sins but then Jesus saved us by His grace, quickening us, giving us eternal life, and we were raised to walk in newness of life. What a wonderful revival! The moment when Jesus saved our hell-bound soul and clothed us in mercy and gave us eternal hope and life in Him! Maybe our first step to revival is for us to remember the first revival that took place in our own lives!

So many times we look at the historical revivals and wish for something as popular and grand as that, but the grandest revival of all time was when Jesus reached down from heaven and saved mine and your soul! I believe that if we remember the grace and love that we were shown at that moment of our salvation and if we let it change our crying into rejoicing, our complaining into praising, and our routine into excitement, then God will revive our hearts and maybe even those around us! When the people in the grocery store or the people at choir practice or your family members start to see and hear about what God has done in your life, both past and present, they will begin to wonder what He can do in theirs!

We all need to shine and remember the greatest revival of all time, and we must not forget that there is good news for every single whosoever!

Whatever excuse you may come up with for not letting God's good news change your life, I guarantee you no excuse will stand in that day when we stand before God, expecting to hear "Well done, thou good and faithful servant" but never hearing it, because we made excuses for not sharing the good news.

A preacher once said, "You can't give hope if you don't have hope." And this is very true! You can't share the good news with others if you haven't claimed it for yourself. Claim God's gift of salvation to you right now if you haven't already, and let the revival start in you!

Philippians 2:15–16; Romans 10:9; Psalm 51:10; Romans 6:4

Our Heavenly Father

On Father's Day, we honor our fathers and thank them for all that they do for us. We tell them we love them more than once, and we make an effort to spend time with them and maybe even give them a gift.

As we take notice of our earthly father, may we not forget that we have a Heavenly Father Who does more for us than our earthly father could ever do, and He is the One Who gave us our earthly father.

Not only does our Heavenly Father shower us with blessings but He provides for our needs and loves us so much that He sacrificed His only Son to pay for our wrongs. God sent us His Holy Spirit to guide and comfort us, and the Father is ever-so-ready to hear our prayers!

He wants to hear from you this Father's Day and not just once a year, but every day. Every problem that we face in life, He has the answer to. All we have to do is communicate.

Some of us have fathers who are no longer with us in person, but we remember them and their influence in our lives. May I just remind you that our Heavenly Father is eternal and He never sleeps and cannot die. Much more than that, He is the Giver of life, and we are alive because of Him, and we have eternal life because of His sacrifice for us!

Just as our earthly fathers help us in our everyday life, so does our Heavenly Father. Here are just a few examples of what each of our fathers does for us:

Earthly father

- fixes physical things for us,
- protects us as best he can,
- works to provide our physical needs,
- corrects us when we do wrong,

- loves us so much,
- leads us to Jesus.

Heavenly Father

- fixes spiritual things for us,
- protects us from unseen enemies,
- provides all our needs,
- corrects us when we do wrong,
- loves us more than we can understand,
- is always watching us.

Your Heavenly Father wants to hear from you, so let today be the day you call out to Him with thanksgiving and love.

John 3:16; Proverbs 3:11–12; 1 Corinthians 8:6; Ephesians 1:3; Isaiah 64:8; James 1:17; 2 Corinthians 1:3–4; John 14:26

Pressures

To the high school senior whose passions and dreams are more than the stars above yet doesn't have peace about going to college like everyone else is advising them to do and to everyone else out there waiting for an answer from God of what to do next…

Don't get discouraged. Jesus knows the desires of your heart, and His plan for your life is greater than all your expectations.

The Lord doesn't want you to be upset and angry because you're clueless as to how to answer all the questions in your head.

The pressures of the world around us are crashing in, and we feel like we've been hit by a truck, as we stumble off to the side of the road, to ask God once again, "What do *You* want me to do?"

Our hearts are overwhelmed by our friends' expectations, our family's hopes for our future, and even our own thoughts and desires of what our life should look like. The struggle is real, but so is God's plan for you. Just because you don't see what it is yet doesn't mean He doesn't have a plan for your life. His plan for your life is far better than you can imagine!

God has blessed you with people who love you enough to take interest in your life and who want to be there to help you. I know it seems like all they want to do is pressure you into doing something you don't want to do, but most likely the truth is that they are just trying to help as best they know how.

Everyone is different, so not everyone will do the same thing or follow the same path as others have. Just keep your eyes fixed upward in hope and in joy, because you know that God has a plan. Remember that the joy of the Lord is your strength and He has not left you. Even in the silence, His hand is still holding on to yours. Talk to Him, and grow close to Him in this time of waiting.

Ask God to show you His will for your life, and follow it.

I'm not saying find out what God wants your life to be like from now until five years down the road, but ask God to show you what step He wants you to take next. And when He opens the door, go follow His plan for your life. This may take a while before you hear the doorknob turn, but until it happens, serve God in the hallway, as the saying goes. Remember your purpose is to praise God and bring Him all the glory, whether that means sitting at His feet and learning to love Him more and more or whether that means going into the unknown doorway of God's path for you.

No matter what, never let the pressures of the world around you hinder your praise to the God Who leads you every day and is slowly turning the key to your next new adventure.

Jeremiah 29:11–13; 1 Timothy 4:12; Proverbs 3:5–6; Proverbs 19:21; Joshua 24:15; Ecclesiastes 12:1

Parted Waters

Soon after the children of Israel saw God's deliverance from the slavery they were in, in Egypt, they faced another problem. They had reached the deep and wide Red Sea, and they knew there was no way they could make it across before the mad Egyptians caught up with them.

Once the Israelites saw there was no possible way of escape, they complained. But Moses, with his faith in the God of the impossible, told the people not to fear but to stand still and watch God's deliverance once again!

Just as expected, God told Moses what to do, and God parted the uncrossable waters, allowing His children to cross over on dry land!

Imagine, as the children of Israel walked between the two walls of water, held up by the mighty hand of God, they probably saw some beautiful deep-sea fish and maybe even stuck their hand on those great walls of water, remembering how they had just murmured against God and doubted what He could do!

What marvelous power they experienced that day as they saw God prove His omnipotence left and right (literally)! Not only did they see God bring them out of Egypt and not only did they walk across the Red Sea on dry land and not only did they see their enemies drowned in those same waters but they saw the leading hand of God in the pillar of cloud and of fire!

The children of Israel saw God's deliverance, His path of provision. They saw God's protection, and they were led by His guidance! This miraculous power of God that was proven to the Israelites time and time again is still proven to us today in the times when we reach the impossibles on our journey!

So many times when we see an uncrossable sea in front of us, we, too, complain and doubt God's purpose for bringing us out into our wilderness! But just as God used the wilderness for the Israelites, to show His power, to prove that they could trust Him, and to teach them to live in daily dependence on God's provision and guidance, God wants to use your wilderness to draw you closer to Him.

He gave the children of Israel the need for food and water in that barren desert, and then He provided water out of a rock and manna out of the morning dew! The point is sometimes God gives us needs just so that He can meet them. He loves it when His children thank Him and recognize that He holds all the power and all the love toward His children.

God's grace is sufficient not only to meet our every need but to bring us into the land He has promised us in the end. Heaven is our destination, and we are led there by God's own hand! The only way we can get into heaven is by accepting that the blood of Jesus is the only thing that could pay for our sins and nothing that we can do is enough to even hide our sins or yet alone pay for them!

Sometimes, we complain about the difficulty of the path in front of us, or we complain that we must humble ourselves before God in order to admit we need a Savior. But despite our complaining, we have every reason to stop complaining and stand still and see the salvation of the Lord!

How will you respond when you reach your uncrossable waters?

Will you complain like the children of Israel did, or will you be like Moses, who with complete confidence in the Lord said, "Fear ye not, stand still, and see the salvation of the Lord, which he will shew to you to day"?

Exodus 14:13; Philippians 4:20; Psalm 78; Acts 4:12

The God of Variety

Throughout all creation, there are so many different creatures, weather characteristics, landscapes, and people, all with different shapes, sizes, and colors!

Isn't it amazing how God works in various ways, yet He is a God Who never ever changes?

Every day, we rely on God to provide our needs, to keep us healthy, to protect us, and to guide us in the path He designed for our life. And He does all that in very different ways. For some people, He provides the job to work for their first car; and for others, He works out a way so that they are simply given a car.

Some people have a big family, while others struggle to have a little one.

There are people who go through cancer and other frustrating illnesses, yet God provides the grace and the strength to get through it for His glory and honor, while others live in perfect health and are able to do so much because they don't have to go to the doctor every few days.

God's plan for your life may be similar to God's plan for your neighbor, but just like no two snowflakes are alike, you are living a life that God has designed just for you. And sometimes we need to take a step back and realize that what God has someone else doing right now, He may not want you to do right now.

When God sees a heart that is willing to do whatever He wants, He blesses that with peace and direction. The direction may not all come at once like it does for other people, but when God does give you direction in what to do next, He doesn't leave you to do it yourself. But rather He helps you through each step of it, walking this path with you hand in hand, if you'll let Him.

Because of how magnificent and awesome God is, even though He never changes, He is never boring! His power and greatness is far beyond our comprehension, and in this ever-changing world, we can lean on our constant and solid hope, Jesus Christ!

The same God Who made the colorful varieties of the fish, birds, land animals, plants, seasons, and places is the very same God Who created you and me!

He cares so much for you. And He wants you to bring your cares, your dreams, your passions, and your desires to Him! 1 Peter 5:7 is a great reminder of this, and we should come before God with our cares not in the mindset that the only thing God is, is a burden bearer but He is a loving and caring God Who not only wants to take your heavy load but wants to give you a lighter load that is full of His plan for you and His blessings and desires for your precious life! There are so many various, beautiful, and life-changing things the Lord wants to give you, if you'll just accept them and give over your own plan and desires for your life. His plan for you is not at all to harm you, but His plan is for you to come closer and closer to the source of true and lasting joy, and that is Himself.

The Lord loves you so much! You are far more valuable to Him than all His creation, which is why He made a way for *you* to spend eternity in heaven with Him!

How amazing it is that the God of variety cares for you! He will always be your steady and constant and your strong rock and your Best Friend, if you'll let Him. No matter what you've done, His grace is enough to cover it completely. And once you ask Jesus into your heart, you are sealed with His Holy Spirit of promise Who can never leave you, and you will *forever* be saved!

Ephesians 1:13; Jeremiah 29:11; 1 Peter 5:7; Isaiah 41:13; Proverbs 3:5–6; Psalm 37:4–5

Unto Us

As Christians, we are all familiar with what the real meaning of Christmas is. It is to celebrate the birth of our Lord and Savior, Jesus Christ! This wonderful time of the year should not only fill the air around us, but it should fill our hearts with joy and gratitude to remember why our Savior came as a baby.

He was born with a purpose, just as you and I were born with a purpose. We were born to glorify God and to share the good news of salvation's love and liberty with those around us! Jesus Christ was born willingly, for the purpose of dying for the sins of the world!

The hope that was brought when our Savior was born is the hope that still lives today! Without Jesus, we were all destined to pay the wages of our sin with eternal death and punishment in hell, but oh what hope we were given when God's only Son found enough love in His heart to step down from heaven into a sin-cursed and wicked world, knowing He would die our death on the cross to pay the full price of our sins! He was innocent; we were guilty. Yet He chose to die for the sins of the world, giving us the eternal hope of heaven!

Isaiah 9:6 begins with this, "For unto us a child is born, unto us a son is given."

Jesus Christ was given to us. He was born to die for our sins. He desires to give us the free gift of eternal salvation, if we'll only trust in Him!

We were given hope. May we remember to not only hold on to this hope that we as Christians have in Christ, but may we also share it with the world around us, shining as we ought to for the glory of God. Jesus was given not only to us but unto every single whosoever, and they need to be reminded that He is their only hope of eternal life.

As I was ironing something the other day, I could feel the intense heat coming from the bottom of the iron. Without even touching it,

I knew it was hot, and I did not want to get my hand up against it or even near it for too long because I knew it would hurt immensely. After feeling that distant heat, I was reminded of the heat that is far, far worse than that of a simple iron even in its hottest temperature. But there is a place where the fire is never quenched, never dies, and never liberates a soul from its eternal wrath and torment.

I am so glad that I will never feel the flames of hell or the torment and pain that fills that place that I deserve! I have complete confidence that I am saved by the blood of Jesus Christ alone and that my eternal destination is in heaven and it is only by the faithful grace of God that I am saved and free from the eternal wages of my own sin!

That's why Jesus came! To free us from that terrible place of torment that we in ourselves had no way out of! Without the shedding of His innocent blood, we would never know the love and grace that His salvation gives! He came for us! He came to us. And He came to free us from the chains of our sin, guilt, and hell! What amazing love that He gave us His life, His everything, and His love that night in Bethlehem!

May we rejoice this Christmas season and in all the days of the years to come that Jesus Christ came to save us and give us eternal life, if only we would call on His name!

Psalm 33:22; Luke 2:10; Luke 2:20; Matthew 5:16

Psalm 71:23
My lips shall greatly rejoice
when I sing unto thee; and my
soul, which thou hast redeemed.

Called to Shine

The second letter of Paul to the Corinthians 4:3 says, "But if our gospel be hid, it is hid to them that are lost."

We read this verse many times, but do we truly realize the sincerity of these words?

We are called to be lights in this dark world. As Christians, who have been saved by the blood of the Lamb and who have forgiveness of sins and peace with God, we are to shine forth the light of His glorious gospel to the people around us!

Every one of us knows people at work. We have family members and even church friends who are living in the darkness of this world. They are blinded. But we have the light and the freedom that they need! We are called to shine!

The world tells us to shine of our own glory, but the Bible tells us to shine of the glory of God!

I think it's interesting how verse 4 says, "the light of the glorious gospel of Christ." Most of the time, we think the adjective *glorious* is describing the light, but it's really describing the gospel! The gospel we have is glorious!

We have a glorious gospel of salvation that is only found in Christ and only accomplished through His finished work on the cross! We need to share that with others, because it is everything they need to be saved, forgiven, and delivered from the great judgment coming!

As Christians, we are not only delivered from eternity in hell, but we are going to be delivered from the tribulation on this earth and all the heartache that the lost people will have to go through! We have the light of the glorious gospel in our hearts, but we must not let its boundaries stop within our hearts, but rather we should let it shine forth unto the people around us who need hope and who need deliverance!

And God said, Let there be light: and there
was light. (Genesis 1:3)

We see right in the very beginning of God's love letter to us that
after God created the heavens and the earth, the very next thing that
God created was light.

Today, we can look around and see people reacting in fear. We
see people yielding their hearts to the enemy, because their faith is
weaker than the pressures this world has pressed upon us all. I believe
that it is a daily choice to walk in fear or to live in faith.

By starting each day in fellowship with God, we choose to submit our anxieties before Him, and we acknowledge and are reminded
through His Word that He alone is in control and that He always has
the final word! We can rejoice in our Savior, our Deliverer, and our
Light! And we should share the light with everyone around us!

2 Corinthians 4:3–4; Psalm 64:1; Psalm 27:1–6; Psalm 18:28;
Matthew 5:15–16; Luke 8:16; Romans 13:12; Philippians 2:15–16

Our Call to Victory!

Unlike many people's thinking today, it is wrong to coerce someone into doing something. Just like people should not be forced or threatened to get vaccinated, people should not be forced to get saved.

Many religions use coerciveness to make people say a prayer or to confess their sins to a priest, or even to get baptized, in order to please the religious crowd. But God's Word says that salvation is not of the law but of grace through the faith of Jesus Christ.

The world is in despair and fear right now, because of something that is out of their control. People think that if they can just stay safe from this virus, then they will be happy and at peace, but the Bible tells us that fear bringeth torment and that peace is only found in the Lord Jesus.

When we walk through the grocery store, do people see something different about us? Do they sense the peace that dwells in our hearts? Or do they sense the same fear that they have of getting sick and possibly dying?

God never intended for His children to fall into Satan's trap of fear. He gave us His Word and everything that we need, to avoid getting snatched into the devil's carefully set snare. But if a soldier has a firearm in his hands but never points it at the enemy, he can only expect to get hit by his adversaries and most likely die without even putting up a fight.

As Christians, our Commander has already won the victory, but do we choose to live in that victory? If we choose to keep our head in the sand, fearing the fiery darts of the wicked, and we never shoot back with confidence, we are neglecting one of the greatest blessings of our salvation—living in victory!

We are in control of how we react to the situations around us! Are we really going to choose to wake up every morning under the oppression of the enemy?

If righteousness exalteth a nation, then wickedness will certainly bring judgment upon a nation.

Why should God honor a coercive society who is all for wickedness and control and who for the most part is against God? People want control because they can't accept the fact that God is the only One Who is in complete control! People want to control God, and the devil thinks that if he can control God's children, then he can control God. No one can tame God or make God obey man's commands. God is the One Who created everyone and everything, and He can use it as He wants.

Because of God's love, He does not force salvation upon anyone, but He graciously and patiently extends it to all, longing for all to accept it. Unfortunately, not all will accept this free and marvelous gift, but so many shove it away in disrespectful rejection. If only they knew that for all eternity, they would be wishing they would have accepted God's mercy!

It grieves the heart of God to watch people reject His sacrifice for them, but I believe it also grieves His heart to watch His very own redeemed children run around like chickens with their heads cut off, living in fear of the very thing they've been set free from! The day you and I accepted Christ as our personal Savior was the very day the Holy Spirit came to live within our hearts, ministering peace, comfort, and joy to our troubled hearts in this fallen world.

Oftentimes, we reject the peace that He wants to give us in our daily lives. We accept God's grace and free gift of eternal life in heaven, but we neglect the peace and the victory He longs for us to live in! Yes, through Jesus Christ our Savior, we have peace with God because Jesus is our righteousness and our Mediator. But God wants us to live the life of peace He intended for us to enjoy daily.

These are sad days, because the time is drawing nearer when the time of grace will end and the time of judgment will come to all the earth. Christians will be delivered through the rapture, but until that day of our deliverance, what will we choose to do? Will we choose to live in fear and in submission to the enemy's threats, or will we choose to stand and fight with our Bibles raised high and our hearts filled with peace and our faces full of the evidence of the joy and faith we have in Christ Jesus?

All of us can rightfully say we should pray more and read the Bible more and share the gospel with more people, but more than anything, we should show God how much we love Him, by allowing Him to have full place in our lives. Today is our call to victory! Today we can live in peace!

Romans 8:15; Romans 13:11; Ephesians 6:10–18; 2 Corinthians 4:6; John 3:7; 1 John 4:10; Hebrews 13:6; Isaiah 26:3; John 14:27; Exodus 14:14; Ephesians 5:16; Galatians 3:3; Galatians 2:16; Galatians 1:3–5; Psalm 98; 1 Corinthians 15:52–58; Romans 5:1; 2 Corinthians 13:11; Philippians 4:4–9; Colossians 3:15; 1 Thessalonians 4:13–18; Luke 16:22–31

Not We Ourselves

Psalm 100:3 says, "Know ye that the Lord he is God: it is he that hath made us, and not we ourselves; we are his people, and the sheep of his pasture."

It is said of many people today that they are self-made, meaning that they can get along by themselves, they are independent, and they created their own circumstances with the sweat of their brow. It may be true that they have worked hard to get where they are today, whether that be a job position, financial position, or even just emotional stability. But no matter how hard we work for something, God is the One Who gives it to us. Some people do their job to the best of their ability and still get fired because of someone else's mistake. Others make a name for themselves by earning degrees and recognition, but the only way that man is who he is, is because of God.

Psalm 100 is a psalm of praise. We should praise God that we don't have to rely on ourselves and we don't have to place upon ourselves the things that only God can do best. In our own sufficiency, we can do nothing when compared with what God can do and what God wants to do for each one of us.

You may think the nest you're building is pretty great, but once you let God build you a birdhouse, you will see just how much you need Him and His powerful provision.

We have someone to lean on through life, someone Who is always there for us and Who wants to communicate with us as we walk through life leaning up against Him. In spite of what some may think, Jesus is not a crutch. He is our legs. He is our Creator, our Sustainer, our Provider, our help, and our health.

Just like an artist knows every little detail about his painting, so the Creator knows every little detail about His creation! God knows the sin nature of man, and Proverbs 15:3 states, "The eyes of the Lord are in every place, beholding the evil and the good." Despite God's omniscience of every man's sin and knowing that man likes to do things his own way rather than God's way, any blessing that we have comes from God and His grace. Have you ever stopped just to think about how gracious God is to you? I have, but not nearly as often as I should. When we stop looking at the blessings in front of us and start looking to the source of the blessings, we feel overwhelmed by the goodness of God, to shower upon us such blessings of which all of us are unworthy!

By humbling ourselves and recognizing how great God is to us, we give the glory to Whom it belongs. Man's purpose is to bring God glory, and when we do that, we find that God blesses us even more. It pleases God to bless His children, but it pleases Him even more when His children give Him praise for all He has done and for all He is!

No man, saved or unsaved, is self-made. But every one of us was created by God and sustained by God, and one day we will be face-to-face with God, but it is up to us to decide if we will be at peace with God. Romans 5:1 says, "Therefore being justified by faith, we have peace with God through our Lord Jesus Christ."

Do you have Jesus as your peace?

Have you given the praise to Whom it belongs?

Psalm 100; Psalm 29:2; Psalm 34:8; Psalm 68:19; Ephesians 1:3, 7; Philippians 2:10–11; Psalm 42:11; Psalm 124:8; Psalm 107:9; Revelation 4:11; Philippians 4:19; Ephesians 2:14

Claiming the Victory

In a world where depression is at every corner, we can be thankful that this world is not our home and that even through the midst of the tumult of fear and anxiety in our minds, we can claim the victory we have in Jesus Christ!

When people isolate themselves from all the blessings God has given them, such as church, family, and friends, they don't realize how much they're isolating themselves from the blessings God has for them in those people! There is spiritual strength and renewal in getting together with fellow believers. So why would we rob ourselves of those blessings by staying home where we have been deceived into thinking is "safe"?

God has promised that He will never leave us. God's Word assures us that nothing can isolate us from Him nor Him from us. His love remains constant, and His presence is all around us, if we would just stop to look for Him.

Our victory is in Jesus Christ, and when we fix our eyes and our hope on Him, we can easily claim the victory that is ours, by living in the blessings and joy of the Lord! Victory is ours, but do we claim it?

Are we thankful for the victory we have in Christ? By not acknowledging it, we are not only being unthankful for it, but we are rejecting it by not grasping onto it and letting it transform our lives.

Today, I'm reminded of the song that we so often sing with strong voices and a mindset of praise, yet when the song is done, do we make an effort to praise God for the victory He's given us by applying it to our everyday lives? Below are the lyrics to that old hymn, and I pray that it ignites a desire in all of us to start claiming the victory we have in Jesus!

Victory in Jesus
E. M. Bartlett

Verse 1
I heard an old, old story how a Savior came from glory,
How He gave His life on Calvary to save a wretch like me;
I heard about His groaning, of His precious blood's atoning,
Then I repented of my sins and won the victory.

Chorus
O victory in Jesus, my Savior, forever!
He sought me and bought me with His redeeming blood;
He loved me ere I knew Him, and all my love is due Him.
He plunged me to victory beneath the cleansing flood.

Verse 2
I heard about His healing, of His cleansing pow'r revealing
How he made the lame to walk again and caused the blind to see;
And then I cried, "Dear Jesus, come and heal my broken spirit,"
And some sweet day I'll sing up there the song of victory.

Chorus
O victory in Jesus, my Savior, forever!
He sought me and bought me with His redeeming blood;
He loved me ere I knew Him, and all my love is due Him.
He plunged me to victory beneath the cleansing flood.

Verse 3
I heard about a mansion he has built for me in glory,
And I heard about the streets of gold beyond the crystal sea;
About the angels singing and the old redemption story,
And some sweet day I'll sing up there the song of victory.

Chorus
O victory in Jesus, my Savior, forever!
He sought me and bought me with His redeeming blood;
He loved me ere I knew Him, and all my love is due Him.
He plunged me to victory beneath the cleansing flood.

Morning Will Come

There are days when I feel strong, and there are days when I feel weak.

On those days when I feel as though mountains move at every word of praise that echoes between the music playing and my singing, faith comes naturally, joy overflows, and music floods the air around me as I know the day is bright and morning has come!

Other days, I feel so weak that I don't think I can get through the day without sitting in a corner with silence in the air. When I try to pray, the words don't come. When I try to sing, the music fails. And when I keep sitting in the silence, thoughts of despair and discouragement crowd my head, leaving room only for tears.

As hard as it is to lift my hands in praise and in faith, on days like these, my heart still knows the goodness of God. And even though my heart is broken, His presence with me doth continually dwell. Even in the silence, I know He is there. Even in the tears, I can hear Him cry with me and call for me to believe that no problem is too hard for God and no mountain is too tall for Him to help me climb and no pain is too deep that He cannot heal, nor is there any impossibility that He cannot work a miracle through to make it possible.

Today may be your strong day, or today may be your weak day. But no matter how you feel right now, please know that God is right there with you and He cares for you and He will help you through the happy times and the sad times. Hold His hand in your silent corner. Rejoice with Him on your best day ever. No matter your circumstances, God hears your heart, and He knows everything that fills your head right now.

We are encouraged in Psalm 30:5 when it says, "Weeping may endure for a night, but joy cometh in the morning." Morning always comes, and just like the morning of Jesus's glorious resurrection, there is great joy in every morning!

Let your weary or jubilant heart be comforted and uplifted by the words to this wonderful hymn:

> Because He lives, I can face tomorrow.
> Because He lives, all fear is gone.
> Because I know He holds the future,
> And life is worth the living,
> Just because He lives!

Counting My Blessings

Abigail Nispel

The sun has set, the stars appear,
The moon gives light to those out there,
Searching for shelter from the cold,
A place of refuge from the storm.
While sheltered I sit in my room so warm,
Cozy in blankets and safe from the storm,
With a cup of tea and soft music playing,
Reading my Bible and quietly praying,
"Lord, why did You see fit to bless me so?
I'm safe from the wind, the rain, and the cold,
Spending this sweet time with You, my Best Friend,
While others out there sit alone with no bed.
Why You bless me, I'll never understand,
But I'll just thank You and praise You with all that I am."

To God be the glory!

About the Author

Sixteen-year-old Abigail Nispel found herself struggling with the reality that she lived thousands of miles away from her family back home, as her family had moved to Romania as missionaries. As time went on, she searched for ways to find the joy in life and a way to gain strength for this time of her life. She tried mastering the language, making new friends, singing in the choir, and taking up photography. But nothing compared to how Jesus could fulfill her soul!

Although she got saved when she was five years old, she never really made time to spend in her walk with God—until now.

During those five years, she found herself waking up every morning thankful that Jesus was her Best Friend and spending a lot of time by her bed, studying her Bible, and pouring her heart out to the Lord, which put a continual song in her heart! Throughout this time of drawing closer to Jesus, she wanted so much to share what God had encouraged her with, so she created a devotional blog. God used it to nurture her heart as well as those she shared it with, but just as Ecclesiastes 3:1 says, "To every thing there is a season." This, too, had a season. Three years went by, and her website was shut down, but that only opened the door to another big opportunity! Praise the Lord that through many faithful prayer warriors and the gracious provision of God Almighty, the many devotional articles on her blog form this book you're holding!

Abigail's prayer for this book is that it is used of God to strengthen, encourage, and speak to your heart in a personal way that brings Him glory and honor!

CPSIA information can be obtained
at www.ICGtesting.com
Printed in the USA
BVHW090016130223
658018BV00006B/14